Australia

Globalizing Regions

Globalizing Regions offers concise accounts of how the nations and regions of the world are experiencing the effects of globalization. Richly descriptive yet theoretically informed, each volume shows how individual places are navigating the tension between age-old traditions and the new forces generated by globalization.

Australia
Anthony Moran

Forthcoming:

Ireland
Tom Inglis

Morocco
Shana Cohen and Larabi Jaidi

The Koreas
Charles Armstrong

China and Globalization
Douglas Guthrie

On Argentina and the Southern Cone
Alejandro Grimson and Gabriel Kessler

Global Iberia
Gary McDonogh

Global Hong Kong
Gary McDonogh and Cindy Wong

Australia

Nation, Belonging, and Globalization

ANTHONY MORAN

ROUTLEDGE   New York • London

A volume in the *Globalizing Regions* series.

Published in 2005 by
Routledge
270 Madison Ave.
New York, NY 10016
www.routledge-ny.com

Published in Great Britain by
Routledge
2 Park Square
Milton Park, Abingdon
Oxon OX14 4RN U.K.
www.routledge.co.uk

10   9   8   7   6   5   4   3   2   1

Library of Congress Cataloging-in-Publication Data
  Moran, Anthony
       Australia: nation, belonging, and globalization / Anthony Moran.
          p. cm. — (Globalizing regions series)
       Includes bibliographical references and index.
       ISBN 0-415-94496-1 (hardback : alk. paper) — ISBN 0-415-94497-X (pbk. :
  alk. paper)
       1. Group identity—Australia. 2. Pluralism (Social sciences)—Australia.
       3. Globalization—Social aspects. 4. Australia—Emigration and immigration.
       5. Australia—Social conditions—21st century. I. Title. II. Series.

  HN843.5.M65 2004
  303.4'0994—dc22   2004009865

For my parents, Bernard and Patricia Moran

Acknowledgments

Charles Lemert provided invaluable help and encouragement in the early stages of formulating this book. My commissioning editor, Dave McBride, saw it through from start to finish. Staff and colleagues at the Centre for Critical Theory, University of the West of England, Bristol listened to and commented upon some of the ideas as they began to take shape. In particular, I thank the Centre's Director, Anthony Elliott, for his intellectual stimulation and friendship, and the Leverhulme Trust for providing the research fellowship that enabled me to spend time at the Centre. James Walter and Judith Brett read and commented on the manuscript, suggesting important improvements. The Australian Research Council has generously provided me with a fellowship and a Discovery Grant that made this book possible. I am greatly indebted to my collaborators on the *Understanding a Changing Australia* project, funded by the Australian Research Council (Reference number DP0343870), from which most of the interviews discussed in the book have been drawn: Judith Brett, Uldis Ozolins, and Guinever Threlkeld. My interpretation and understanding of what our interviewees were saying have been stimulated and expanded by my collaboration and discussion with these colleagues. I have also used interviews gathered, in the late 1980s, for the *Images of Australia* project at the University of Melbourne, funded by the Australian Research Grants Commission (Reference number A58716358). One of the directors of that research, John Cash, generously allowed our research team access to this important archive of interviews. I am indebted to those who conducted and coordinated this research: John Cash, Alan Davies, Graham Little, and the interviewers employed by this project to conduct interviews. It goes without saying that I could not have written this book without the many people who gave up their time to be interviewed. I cannot name them; but I thank them for their generosity and for sharing their thoughts and feelings with me. La Trobe University's School of Social Sciences, and in particular the Politics Program, has been a wonderful environment in which to write this book. In particular, I thank Liz Byrne and Nella Mete for their administrative support.

Finally, I wish to thank, as always, Claudia and Liam, and my extended family.

Australia is a nation born of globalization, a fragment of an empire in the New World. A largely immigrant country of approximately 20 million divided federally into six states and two territories, it is united under a national government based on British and American constitutional and parliamentary principles and traditions. It is the first and only nation spanning an entire continent, some $7,692,000 \text{ km}^2$, 70 percent of it semi-arid to arid land (Australian Bureau of Statistics 2003). Its carriage first hitched to Britain from which it was born, and now to the United States, the New World nation it once hoped to emulate; Australia nervously watches its region, and the rest of the world, as it attempts to charter its way through the second century of its existence as a nation.

How far back should we go when we start talking about globalization? Does it date from the Roman Empire and the trading and cultural links that it created? Does it begin around 1500 when Europeans first colonized other parts of the world, far beyond European frontiers? Does it begin in the twentieth century with the explosion of technological means of transport and communication? Was the world more global during the period of high imperialism? I cannot pretend to answer these larger questions in this book. In any case, they have been comprehensively addressed elsewhere. Held et al. (1999) view globalization as a series of waves of activity: different historical periods have witnessed more globalization in some domains and less in others, stretching far back in history. Globalization, they point out, is a very long story. My intention is more modest, and indeed more specifically focused on Australia. This book emphasizes the *intensification*, *transformation*, and *modification* of globalizing processes in Australia that do, indeed, stretch back a long way.

The history of globalization in Australia begins in 1788. Some might argue that it begins earlier, with the migrations of indigenous peoples into the continent between 40,000 and 60,000 years ago, according to current archeological evidence (Flood 1999; Lourandos 1997). (On the other hand, many indigenous people dispute the idea that their ancestors migrated to Australia, claiming that they have always been here.) The year 1788 is chosen because it is actually then that the mythical land of the south, which had exercised the minds of Europeans long before it was ever "discovered," begins to be affected by the global movements that emerged around the fifteenth century with the expansion of Europe under the impact of capitalism. When the tall ships with their convicts and officers first entered what is now Sydney Harbour, indigenous peoples had lived and developed their societies and cultural systems for at least 40,000 years on the Australian land mass. There is evidence of trade and interaction between indigenous people and voyagers from Asia in the north of Australia, of some contact with the Dutch whose vessels were blown onto the North West coast en route to the Spice Islands, and with other explorers such as William Dampier, before the eighteenth century, but the bigger story is of separation from the rest of the world until the British decided to settle a penal colony.

Australia began its modern phase as a nation–continent of mostly white British settlements in a region vastly unlike it, ethnically, religiously, and in terms of social organization. In the early part of the twentieth century, Australia saw itself as a democratic white British outpost in a colonized region yet to experience the impact of democratization and modern economic development. Having largely decimated and silenced its indigenous peoples, it was a culture of dislocation, seeking security and identity in the embrace of Empire. By the end of the nineteenth century, settlers had transformed the Australian landscape, introduced flora and fauna from "home," and in so doing had displaced indigenous landscapes and meanings built up over thousands of years. For many, "home" was a complex notion that combined remembered or recounted images of Britain with a developing sense of Australia and its uniqueness.

One of the stories told by some Australians about Australia is that it was, until the 1980s, a society closed into itself, sheltered from the world and its problems. This was exemplified by the "insular" Australian settlement negotiated by the various competing political factions in the early part of the twentieth century, underpinned by a wide policy of protection, which remained in effect until the Hawke Labor government of the 1980s finally broke it open (Kelly 1992). The five pillars of this "Australian Settlement," according to Kelly, were White Australia, Industry Protection, Wage Arbitration, State Paternalism, and Imperial Benevolence (i.e., cultural and economic development and military protection under Britain's wing). Many scholars and popularizers writing about Australia's history and present conditions have taken this understanding on board. According to Kelly, much of this settlement had to be dismantled because of the imperatives of globalization (see also Kelly 2001).

A variant of this story, especially evident among overly enthusiastic devotees of a particular brand of multiculturalism, has it that Australia was a homogeneous and boring Anglomorph society until it opened itself, after the Second World War, to non-British European and non-European immigration. According to this view, Australia was, until the impact of its waves of more recent immigrants, an inward-looking and "protected" society, afraid of difference, conservative, cautious, and conformist. Cultural diversity, and opening itself up to the benefits of globalization, so the story goes, made the society more dynamic and worldly.

Like all stories, there is an element of truth and much fiction in these attempts to describe Australia and its history. Australia's short postinvasion history, although it lacks the revolutions and civil wars of other countries, is eventful and inventive nonetheless. Moreover, it is a global story.

Australians, by virtue of their position in the world — in the world economy, geographically — as members of a nation formed by waves and waves of immigration — a product of the former British Empire, now a highly developed but minor player in world affairs — have always had one eye firmly fixed on the outside world. From the beginning, Australians were engaged with the outside world and world events (Meredith and Dyster 1999; Galligan et al. 2001). After all, the early prosperity of the colonies, and then the nation, depended on innovative farming and mining aimed at massive commodity exports. Initially, these flowed overwhelmingly to Britain, for which Australia was a "farm and quarry" economy, but as the twentieth century wore on, Australians produced for more truly international markets, primarily in the United States, Japan, China, and the rest of East Asia (Catley 1996: chap. 9; White 1992: 33).

Australians were involved in wars, many of them far from Australia (the Boer War, the First World War, the Second World War, The Korean and Vietnam Wars), indicating that they always saw their national interests as intrinsically international (originally imperial) or global. They have continued this tradition with their involvement in the two recent Gulf Wars. Internally, Australia's history was hardly settled, complacent, or protected. Australia underwent two major depressions (in the 1890s and the 1930s), experienced major industrial conflicts, major social conflicts over conscription during the First World War and over involvement in the Vietnam War, and major political struggles for workers, women's, and indigenous rights. Admittedly, when compared to the conflicts of twentieth-century Europe, these conflicts seem relatively minor. Apart from the conflict with Aborigines, Australia's internal history has been peaceful.

The link between ethnic diversity and societal dynamism, and, therefore, the assumed link between ethnic homogeneity and cultural stagnation, might be a popular notion for some, but operates from a flawed assumption about the nature of creativity (for a critique, see Hannerz 1996: chap. 5). There is no reason why a society cannot be at the same time culturally and ethnically homogenous *and* creative in politics, the arts, and culture more generally. By the same token, one does not have to subscribe to the view that Australia before the Second World War was stagnant, because it was too Anglomorph to support, even celebrate, the multicultural Australia of the present — an indisputable reality beyond the rhetoric — and to recognize that it has brought new ideas, developments, and even new capacities to Australian society.

Globalization has a special meaning for Australians. Since the 1980s, they have been told by their politicians, economic leaders, and various cultural entrepreneurs and commentators that globalization is the main game and that they had better get used to it. From the 1980s on, Australia has been "opened up," "transformed," "remade," and "reinvented" in order to fit perceived global realities, especially realities of the economic variety.

As I was packing up our flat in the days before leaving for a year of research in Britain, the news came over the radio that Australian authorities had stopped a Norwegian ship, *MV Tampa*, carrying asylum seekers picked up from a stranded vessel that had sailed from Indonesia. Australia's Prime Minister John Howard was quick to reassure the Australian public that under no circumstances would he allow such "illegal immigrants" to enter Australian territory. As I listened to the comments and statements from politicians, the various commentaries from journalists and other interested parties, and to talk back radio, I was struck by the fact that, apparently, these haphazard movements of desperate people were not what was meant when people talked about opening up Australia. If globalization is all about international flows and the freeing up of impediments to such flows — a sort of worldwide open market — then how is one to reconcile this with the increasingly hostile reception to asylum seekers in Australia and in other wealthy countries?

About two weeks later, now at my university in Britain, I was called down from my office to watch, on the big television screen in the student cafeteria, the terrorist tragedy as it unfolded on September 11. With the aid of globalized media networks, and from September 11 onward, al-Qaeda terrorized people all over the world, especially those of the west seen as the most likely targets for future like-minded terrorist raids. In Bristol, where I was staying, the stores soon ran out of gas masks.

September 11, as was so obviously, and almost immediately, apparent, was a world event reverberating far beyond New York. Australia, like the U.S., had its own more direct connections, with one of its citizens, David Hicks, turning up among the terrorist suspects rounded up in Afghanistan and sent for interrogation to Guantanamo Bay. (Just over a year later, 88 Australians were among the 202 people killed in the Bali bombings, another terrorist attack.) September 11 and its aftermath made it clear to everyone just how small the world had become, and how none of us, no matter how hard we tried, could ever again live in splendid isolation.

"Globalization," Held and his coauthors argue at the beginning of their influential opus *Global Transformations*, "may be thought of initially as the widening, deepening and speeding up of worldwide interconnectedness in all aspects of contemporary social life ..." (Held et al. 1999: 2). This seems as good as any starting definition for globalization that I have come across.

The two events just described, the *MV Tampa* incident and September 11, reveal starkly the unavoidable interconnectedness of the world at the beginning of the twenty-first century. Both events touch on the issue of borders. In the case of September 11, borders proved no protection against an unruly, even terrifying world of death and destruction. The event set in train a new global security approach — the war on terror and the notion of the preemptive strike. In the *MV Tampa* case, the Australian government, which had already, like governments before it, given up so much of its control of the economic flows over Australian borders, decided that it must, in other

7 Introduction

ways, protect national borders at all costs. It would make a case for its right, even in the age of globalization, to fiercely control its own borders, to keep the unruly world of people-on-the-move out. In its place would be the orderly movement of peoples decided for and by Australian citizens through their elected representatives. Every government, Prime Minister Howard and his ministers insisted, had the right to decide who entered its shores and under what circumstances and conditions — no matter how desperate they were.[1]

This book is theoretically informed, but is driven by narratives and dense description. It puts everyday experience at the forefront. The attempt is to bring Australia to life for readers both in and outside Australia. The aim is to make readers think again about what place, culture, and tradition mean in the global era.

Since the end of the Second World War, Australia has witnessed dramatic changes. The indigenous resurgence, the transformation of the polity from white British to multiethnic through a postwar program of mass immigration (Betts 1999), the shift from industry protection and centralized industrial relations to more market-based economic relations, and the changing role of the state: these changes have irredeemably altered the social and political landscape. Decolonization and the subsequent economic, cultural, and military rise of Asian and South East Asian states have transformed the region, establishing for Australia increasingly important military and trading partners and competitors. Australia, like all contemporary societies, cannot help but look beyond its own national frontiers and engage with an uncertain world.

The first chapter provides a brief overview of globalization and the debates surrounding this essentially contested concept, and examines the concept and the debates in the light of Australia's history and experiences. I discuss the opening up of Australia economically and culturally in the period since the early 1980s and the impact of neoliberal reforms on the role of the state. Since the early 1980s, Australians have experienced a seismic shift as the state has gradually reoriented itself away from the more obvious guiding role of the past. This has had unsettling implications on the way that people think about Australian society and their place within it. In the final sections of the chapter, I examine the theme of Australian political culture and consider its state under the impact of globalizing pressures and trends.

The second chapter provides a preliminary examination of the fate of Australian national identity in the period of intensifying globalization. National identity is a recurring theme throughout the book. Many theorists of globalization argue that national identity is becoming less important, and less salient for people as the world becomes more global. I argue that this is not the case for Australians. On the other hand, intensifying globalization stimulates new forms of Australian national identity, just as it challenges older forms. This chapter explores different experiences of Australian national identity, and suggests different formative contexts for its production. Through such an exploration, I will show that the relationship between national identity and globalization is not a case of counterpositioning, but is complex.

The large-scale movements of peoples, and the increasingly global nature of such flows (Castles and Miller 1998), are major issues faced by nation-states in the era of globalization. Social spaces throughout the world are now, and increasingly, shared by a diversity of communities, groups, and individuals. Are such spaces still conceivable as national spaces? This new global reality is debated and handled in Australia in ways that reflect its history and traditions. The third chapter explores immigration and the transformation of Australian identity from whiteness to multicultural identity (Castles et al. 1988). Australia is, for the most part, an immigrant society. Until the late 1960s, Australia attempted, quite successfully, to produce and reproduce itself as a "white nation," primarily through the exercise of racially discriminatory immigration policies. A series of processes and events resulted in the gradual breakdown and loss of legitimacy of the white Australia ideal from the 1960s onward. Since then, Australia has repositioned itself as a multicultural nation that accepts and even celebrates its diversity. Although these developments have not been without their critics, the shift has been largely, and even remarkably, successful.

In the fourth chapter, where I examine settler/indigenous relations, I develop another important layer to the understanding of the way that the Australian national community has been transformed through its need to confront forms of diversity and strangeness in the period of intensifying globalization. I explore the terrain of the shift from white Australia and assimilation to Aboriginal self-determination and land rights. I highlight the challenges and dilemmas, and also the possible gains (see, e.g., Tully 1995) involved in such transformations. These include the challenge of rethinking social (and national) space and its meanings for the different peoples of Australia. I will also illustrate the complexity of the relationship between tradition and globalization (Heelas et al. 1996; Beck 1997): not a simple overcoming or dissolving of tradition, but a reinterpretation or reconfiguring of tradition under new conditions.

Reactions to and treatment of refugees and asylum seekers throw into sharp relief the tensions and contradictions of the globalizing experience. In the face of governments advocating free trade as the key to the alleviation of world poverty and to the production of the good life, asylum seekers, refugees, or the so-called economic migrants encounter the politics of fear, resistance, resentment, and from the extreme right, hatred. Questions of national sovereignty are central to debates about asylum seekers, as are questions concerning the capacities of democratic societies to accommodate, rehouse, employ, and integrate refugees. Australia's strategy, including mandatory detention and, more recently, the processing of asylum seekers outside Australian territory, has drawn international attention and condemnation. Chapter Five analyzes the extent to which the Australian reaction parallels, or is a more extreme form of other nations' responses to this issue. The Australian experience is compared with broader global trends.

In choosing the themes for these different chapters, I have kept in mind readers interested in Australia specifically, and those concerned with thinking about processes of globalization more generally, in all of their diversity and with their nuances in different places. While being particularly pertinent to Australian society, these themes reverberate with lived experiences elsewhere. Australian settler/indigenous relations have certain similarities with such relations in the U.S., Canada, New Zealand, Latin America, and many other places. The reformulation of social space, although focused here on Australian realities, is felt across the globe. Multiculturalism is a reality that increasingly characterizes many places, and the problem of asylum seekers and "illegal" immigration is at the forefront of politics in Australia, Europe, and the Americas. The related issue of the transformation of the Australian state and national identity also finds commonalities with other places.

This book adopts a grounded approach to understanding the ways that politics and political change, and the impact of globalization, are experienced and lived. Throughout this book, I make use of indepth interviews conducted by myself and others dating from the late 1980s to the present. The interviews have been conducted with Australians from many different walks of life and geographical and social locations. The many people I have spoken with, or whose interview transcripts I have read, have helped me to understand everyday experiences of globalization: how it touches people's lives, and how they make sense of it. My hope is that I have been able to convey these experiences to readers.

The interviews were conducted at two key points, in the period 1986 to 1990 and from 2002 to the present. They involve more than 300 hours of interviews with approximately 60 men and women. Each participant was interviewed for a total of 6 to 10 hours, over three to five occasions. The interviews were broad in scope, ranging from life history to specific views about the important social cleavages in Australian society, and to perceptions of what were the most pressing issues of the day. The participants were drawn from city, rural, and regional locations. Many of the interviewees referred to themselves as "ordinary" people, and I am happy to characterize them as such here. They are "ordinary" in the sense that, with a few exceptions, they are not prominent public figures, commentators, writers, or politicians crafting their answers for an imagined public, but people talking anonymously about their ideas and feelings about living in Australian society.

The interviews from 1986 to 1990 were conducted by the *Images of Australia* research team at the University of Melbourne. These interviews are now in the possession of the *Understanding a Changing Australia* research team at La Trobe University. Together with the other members of the *Understanding a Changing Australia* research team, I have conducted interviews from 2002 onward. Some of these are with people from the original *Images of Australia* sample, and the remainder are new interviewees. All of the names for interviewees used in the text are pseudonyms.

One

Globalization is a buzzword in the social sciences. It is also a word on the streets that has the power to move people to pitched battle, as occurred across the globe from Seattle and Genoa to Melbourne as the new millennium dawned. A banner at one of Melbourne's antiglobalization protests during 2000 simply read "Stop Globalization," as if one could stop the world from turning, or stop history in its tracks. The everyday understanding of globalization, at least among protesters, seems to be something like the impact of large, anonymous, transnational corporations, on things such as democracy, national economies, workers' wages, consumerism, the environment, and the Third World. The main targets of antiglobalization are economic liberalization — free trade, unhindered capital flows — and the institutions that promote it, for example, the World Trade Organization, the World Bank, and the International Monetary Fund. The antiglobalization protesters also have a cultural argument or complaint: "We don't want to become just like everyone else," protesters seem to be saying. Or, to put a name to it, "we don't want to become American." Probing still further, one senses an argument about sovereignty: "we want to be able to control and direct our own lives in our own places."

Such protests, of course, cannot be considered to reflect the concerns of everyone. They do, however, point to certain anxieties — felt subtly by some, and by others as an overwhelming surge — experienced under the intensification of globalization in the last few decades. One such anxiety is a doubt about the meaning of globalization. Neil, a retired Australian farmer and union man, reflecting on the period since the Second World War, sensed that Australians were going through times of momentous change, but felt that they still did not have the language or the concepts to really help them understand these new circumstances. Governments, he felt, did not know the dimensions of what they were now dealing with either: "I think that the times are not as black and white now. The issues are not as black and white. Globalization is something that parliamentarians don't understand. That ordinary people like us don't understand." Once, politicians, even ordinary people, could get a hold of the system and find ways to work it. You could pull this lever when this problem arose. There were tried and tested ways of doing things. Treasurers could stand up in parliament and deliver budgets without notes. "Now they bring them in on books and books and books. It's a major enterprise. And how can ordinary politicians understand it?"

Another one of these anxieties apparent in Australia concerns the national inheritance. There is a fear among some people that globalization means selling Australia to the highest bidder, without any real thought of the consequences. This has both an emotional, nationalistic aspect, "Australia for the Australians," and a more practical aspect, concerning the perceived loyalties and commitments of companies operating in Australia. The following comments from Mick, a late middle-aged Vietnam veteran, expresses this well:

I can't understand how we can sell Australia. You can't buy a house in Vietnam. You can if you're living with a Vietnamese or married. She can buy it, you can't... . People think Vietnam's a country that hasn't got any brains and can't look after itself. You can't own it. You can't own Thailand. Why in the hell are we selling so much? Why is the government selling? Lease it, rent it, but why sell it?

Reflecting on the local industries that were the lifeblood of his rural community, he was even more troubled:

This mill was owned by Australians and it was making a quid. So bang, it was sold to someone, a British mob. Now it's owned by a New Zealand mob. Now they're extremely worried. This New Zealand mob is a national company and it may pull out of Australia or pull out of here... .

If the mill went, then the whole town would go. Everything else would close down. The message for people like Mick is that you cannot expect foreign companies to feel the same sense of committment to the places where they operate as you would Australian ones, at least not as the latter operated in previous times. Mick and the people he talks to seem to think that Australian companies would be more loyal.

For many in the social sciences, contemporary globalization means a profound set of changes, economic, social, cultural, and political, transforming the experience of time and space, nationhood, and identities. The feeling or sense of being part of a global reality, even if this is experienced in different ways in different places, is of profound significance. It is hard to conceive, for example, any instance where members of a society these days can imagine themselves without having some concept of their place within the broader world. This is also true for the members of those societies who do not enjoy the mixed pleasures of the global superhighway. Even they have access to the proliferation of images, film, television, photographs, billboards etc., that have had such a massive impact on the consciousness and imagination of people across the globe since the latter part of the twentieth century (Appadurai 1996: chap. 3). They are compelled to see themselves as members of a global society, even as they remain brothers and sisters, mothers and fathers, members of religious or ethnic groups, and members of nations. It is certainly true of Australia and Australians.

Contemporary globalization means the intensification of the relationship between local and distant events and sites, the acceleration of the speed with which they impact upon each other, and the permeability of a range of social and political boundaries (with all of the creativity and tension this provokes). It involves processes of detraditionalization, deterritorialization, and the compression of time–space (in other words, the ways that the constraints of distance and time have been eroded by new forms of transport and instantaneous forms of mass communication that result in the reorganization of economic, social, cultural, and political life) (Harvey 1989; Giddens 1990, 1994; Heelas, et al. 1996; Bauman 1998; Held et al. 1999; Held and McGrew 2000). It means the closer intermeshing of economies and increased (and increasingly less constrained) capital flows, the expansion of the capacity for communication, the explosion of media cultures, and processes of both homogenization and reinvention of cultures and identities. Some of the most important features of a globalized society include: Labor flexibility; the shifting of sites of production around the globe and the ramifications of such transfers at the local and national levels; the pressure and desire for populations to shift, in part as a response to the massive disparities of wealth and opportunity between geographical locations generated by globalization, and the intensified awareness due to communications of those disparities; and changes to the ways that states act. Globalization is, as David Held and others have suggested, multifaceted, and must be understood in terms of each of the following facets: economic, cultural, political, legal, military, environmental, and so on (Held et al. 1999).

Theories of globalization have burgeoned over the last decade. Nevertheless, globalization remains an essentially contested concept, expressed in a range of important debates. First, there is an ongoing debate between those who believe that it is primarily mythological (or ideological) and those who believe that it is a new reality with important structural features (Held et al. 1999; Held & McGrew 2000, 2002; Rosenberg 2000). Writers such as Hirst and Thompson (1999) argue that economic integration was in fact more international in the nineteenth century, and that what we call globalization is more accurately seen as intensified internationalization: in other words, that nation-states assert their interests in an international economy, and the more powerful nation-states are better equipped to do so (see also Hirst and Thompson 1995). Others, like Linda Weiss (1998: chap. 6), point out that much of the movement of goods over borders is between different branches of the same transnational companies, and that such movements are far from "global," with most Organization for Economic Cooperation and Development (OECD) countries trading mainly with two or three other countries. A related debate concerns regionalization vs. globalization, or even regionalization as a major feature of globalization. It is true that the exports to GDP ratio in world trade figures increased dramatically after the 1960s, almost doubling in the period from 1960 to 1990. This indicated the growing importance of the international market and increasing "interdependence of the international system." However this development was by no means unprecedented. It is arguable that the period leading up to the First World War was far more global, or "internationalized" as Weiss prefers, in terms of "trade, investment and capital flows" (Weiss 1998: 170). In the new world order post-1989, as the argument goes, the world is increasingly divided into regions of influence — Europe, the Americas, and the Asia-Pacific — following the major financial and trading blocs.

In the post-Second World War period, Australia has gradually shifted its trading emphasis away from Britain and Europe, and toward its own geographical region. Britain's entry into the European Common Market in the early 1970s was one of the major forces contributing to this change in trading relations.[1] This does not, however, indicate an Australian retreat from globalization into regionalism. On the contrary, in a period that has witnessed the setting up of regional economic and power blocs, Australia is in danger of being left out. Australia is outside of the North American Free Trade Agreement, the European Free Trade Association and, closer to home, Australia has been unable to form a free trade agreement for its region with New Zealand and the Association of South East Asian Nations (Capling 2001: 1). It has only very recently (i.e., at the time of writing, in 2004) signed a free trade agreement with the U.S., the implications of which are not yet apparent. This too is a new reality faced by Australians in the age of globalization, with its shifting sites of power and allegiance. Australian trade ministers are well aware of this phenomenon and scout the world searching for markets and trading partners. They and others work with other governments and global bodies to get a better deal for Australia in truly international markets, actively pursuing multilateralism.[2]

The arguments about trade and capital flows and regionalization are primarily about economic globalization, and whatever their merits, they do not falsify the claim that cultural globalization continues apace, that the peoples of the world are coming into closer and closer contact with each other, and are more often, and more intensely, exposed to forms of life other than their own. This gives rise, as Ulf Hannerz has argued, not to a homogenized global culture, nor to "a cultural mosaic, of separate pieces with hard, well-defined edges" (1992: 218) but to a global ecumene, with "fuzzy boundaries" that make it increasingly difficult, and more arbitrary to analytically delimit cultural units.

This suggests another important debate about the impact of globalization on the traditional capacities, roles and activities of the nation-state, and on national identities. Recently, sociologists such as Ulrich Beck (2000, 2002) have written of the redundancy of the nation-state, and of the increasing irrelevance of national identity in an era of globalization, where identities become increasingly cosmopolitan. Talk of this kind is provocative, but seems to me an overstatement of the facts, in both a general sense, and specifically in the case of the Australian experience. Globalization clearly has implications for the role of the state and for national identity and national solidarity; but understanding these implications is no straightforward matter. Some critics have been too quick to sign the nation-state's death certificate in the era of intensified globalization.

What we *can* say with some conviction is that global pressures (i.e., pressures of world trade, pressures from the World Bank and from the International Monetary Fund), perceptions of global realities, and the spread of neoliberal ideologies have meant that state strategies the world over have been transformed in recent decades. Australia is no exception. Held et al. (1999) distinguish three modes of state operation responding to global pressures: (1) the neoliberal minimal state, (2) the developmental state ("government as the central promoter of economic expansion"), and (3) the catalytic state ("government as the facilitator of coordinated collective action"). The adoption of one of these strategies, or more likely a specific combination of all three, is determined by economic, political, social, and cultural contexts. "Rather than globalization bringing about the 'end of the state,'" they argue, "it has encouraged a spectrum of adjustment strategies and, in certain respects, a more activist state" (Held et al. 1999: 9), a position strongly underscored by writers such as Weiss (1998). A more active state is especially evident among the advanced capitalist societies where, although sovereignty and autonomy have been eroded and transformed, the state has found new roles for itself in intergovernmental agreements, negotiation, and regional and global governance (Held et al.1999: 440–441).

Another way of formulating this is to speak of the rise of the new regulatory state in the advanced capitalist countries. Privatization of formerly public services and utilities is complemented by the creation of new regulatory bodies to ensure that the new entities carry out their tasks in a manner expected by democratic polities. Thus, governments remain active but shift their emphasis from rowing to steering (Osborne and Gaebler 1992; Braithwaite 2002).

This debate about state capacities and globalization has a special relevance for Australians who have seen a transformation in the way their own state operates in recent times. Traditionally, the Australian state had been very interventionist. It played a central and fundamental role in the development of Australian society, from the early colonial settlements to the latter part of the twentieth century.

Reasons for this were rooted in Australian history and circumstances. The eminent Australian historian W.K. Hancock (1930: 69) famously argued that a "peculiar" Australian attitude to government arose out of Australia's unique history as a settler society in a region distant from Europe and emerging with a difficult geography and climate. From penal colony onward, Australia could only advance by dint of collective action, and the site of collective action was the state. New societies required "ample government," particularly when the land would, for the most part, support only sparse population settlement. The state was the avenue for collective action of communities of separated, struggling individuals, who, because of their migration, were strangers to each other, and had little cause as individuals to cooperate. Peculiarities of dislocation, distance, and terrain meant that the emerging governing bodies always had to take the leading role in providing the infrastructure for society to develop. The state involved itself in land settlement; it funded and ran the railways and communications, built roads, and created irrigation schemes (Hancock 1930; Eggleston 1932; Davies 1966).

During the nineteenth century, state agencies were responsible for expanding the Australian economy. They did this through funding, supporting, and coordinating mass immigration, and by attracting capital, mainly from Britain. Business enterprises depended on the government to find and attract labor and capital. The developing state built up a large public sector, and was responsible for large-scale public enterprises that employed thousands of Australians (Butlin et al. 1982: chap. 2), a much higher percentage of the workforce than in Britain at the turn of the twentieth century (Aitkin 1986).

From the initial days of the nation (i.e., after the 1901 federation), and even in the colonies in the late nineteenth century, the state was deeply involved in the arbitration of the battles between capital and labor, attempting to provide peaceful and fair solutions to potentially violent conflicts (Bell and Head 1994). The state set about ensuring decent living conditions through guaranteeing, after the famous Harvester Judgement of 1907, and through the Arbitration Court, the "living wage": no family with a working breadwinner would go without the necessities of life.[3] Centralized wage fixation and compulsory arbitration of labor disputes made Australia distinctive in the world. Deakinite "New Protection" meant that manufacturing and other industries would be protected from international competition if they agreed to provide workers with the "living wage" and decent working conditions.

Through the White Australia Policy, adopted as Australia moved toward federation with the widespread support of the general Australian population, the state sought to design the ethnic composition of the emerging nation, and so, as the argument went, ensure national unity and freedom from racial conflict. In addition, the White Australia Policy was meant to maintain the worker's paradise by preventing capital from importing cheap nonwhite labor.

Although the welfare state was not as strong as it was in some developed countries like Germany — Australia did not gain national health care coverage until the 1970s — targeted welfare (i.e., old age pensions) emerged early in the twentieth century, and the welfare state strengthened significantly after the Second World War (Castles 1985; Watts 1980). Free state education, at least at the primary school level, was an achievement of colonies before the turn of the twentieth century. Even before the postwar period, as Francis Castles (1985) has argued, Australia had developed its own distinctive form of wage-workers' welfare state that rivaled the welfare states of Europe in its capacities to ensure that most Australians achieved a decent standard of living.

During the nineteenth and twentieth centuries, through policies of protection, including tariff barriers and the regulation of finance and banking, and through the incentives of infrastructure provision and other industry support, the state played a direct role in supporting and building up Australia's manufacturing industry, thus diversifying a commodity-heavy economy. Although it had considerable retarding effects on competitiveness and efficiency that became increasingly evident in the 1970s and 1980s, industry protection was necessary and instrumental in the industrialization of Australia (Emy 1993: chap. 3).[4] At the same time, and as part of a large-scale compensation package for the protection of industry, Australian governments played a central role in supporting the agricultural sector, especially from the 1920s, with marketing boards, pooling arrangements, and price stabilization (Catley 1996: 52).

The state in Australia, therefore, played an important role in nation-building. This role extended well into the twentieth century, with continued support for the development of the nation's infrastructure (the post Second World War Snowy

Mountains Hydroelectric scheme is emblematic), in the building of the population through state-organized immigration programs, in subsidizing and supporting rural areas so that they did not fall too far behind the cities, and in supporting the social structure through conciliation and arbitration, central wage-fixation, public housing schemes, and other social policies. Through such action, the state was visible to the population as a resource to be engaged with for the betterment of their lives.

The cultural tradition arising from this situation, Hancock argued, was one of individualism underwritten by the state. "Australian democracy," he concluded, "has come to look upon the State as a vast public utility, whose duty it is to provide the greatest happiness for the greatest number" (Hancock 1930: 72). Australians, for the most part, accepted a form of "social liberalism" (Brett 1996) where the state engaged in large-scale projects of social reform and improvement.

From another angle, one can emphasize the way that the Australian state has underwritten and supported national solidarity — people thinking and feeling that they have a stake in the broader society, despite social divisions like class. Australians are not suspicious of the state in the way that Americans are said to be. There is no bill of rights written into the Australian constitution. The very early involvement of the organized labor movement within the structures of the state (in some colonies in the nineteenth century, and federally in the initial years of the twentieth century) added to the belief that the people owned the state and could use it to develop an egalitarian society, free of debilitating poverty.

Much of my discussion of globalization in this book deals with the changes that Australia has undergone since the end of the Second World War. The period of the transformation of the Australian state is even more recent. Although I will not be dealing extensively with the specific details of that transformation, I will be registering its implications, and its impact, throughout the book. Indeed, in any discussion of globalization and Australia, some mention of the transformed role of the state is unavoidable.

From the beginning of the 1980s, and reflecting trends in other western countries (Cox 1997), the adoption of neoliberal models for the organization of the economy and society revolutionized the role of the Australian state (i.e., through deregulation of capital markets; the lowering of tariff protection; privatization of social services and public utilities; decreased public spending; and the dismantling of compulsory arbitration of labor disputes [Kelly 1992; Catley 1996]). These developments are best conceived not as the retreat of the Australian state (Pusey 1991) but as a reorientation in state practice and rhetoric, driven in large part by perceptions, and realities, of the post-1970s global economy.

Australia had always been a trading nation; but most of its export had traditionally been agricultural and mining commodities to Britain, which was also the source of people, capital, and goods. In this sense, although in most other ways an advanced western society, Australia had the economic profile of an unevenly developed, dependent nation — albeit one with a high standard of living for its majority nonindigenous population. From the 1960s, the steep rise of global trading in manufactured goods and services, and steadily declining commodity prices, affected Australia's position in the world economy and, in particular, led to a recurrent crisis in its balance of payments. Governments and economists realized that, if it was to continue to enjoy a high standard of living, Australia would have to become an exporter of manufactured goods and services, and rely less heavily on traditional commodity exports for which there were also new competitors (Emy 1993; Schedvin 1987). This meant that the manufacturing and service industries, previously protected and geared largely to supplying the domestic market, would have to become more competitive and export oriented.

A perception arose in government and public service circles, and among economists and various influential commentators, that Australian culture itself had to change, and that government would have to put certain measures in place to ensure that this happened (see, e.g., Walsh 1979; for an overview, see Emy 1993: chap. 3; for a critique, see Capling et al. 1998: chap. 10). Australians, many argued, had become complacent as a result of being "protected" from the vicissitudes of the world economy. They relied too heavily on the state to sort out their problems. A series of government reports from the late 1980s onward enthusiastically proclaimed that Australians needed to become more entrepreneurial and enterprising if Australia was to retool itself in the globalizing world (Garnaut 1989; Hilmer 1993; Keating 1994; Karpin 1995).

Labor governments, against their own traditions, began to look increasingly to the market to solve the problems of the Australian economy. This economy would become more competitive, the argument went, once governments stepped back and took away the things (like tariffs) that had "artificially" propped up so many enterprises. Direct government involvement in the economy came to be seen as a distorting influence. By being exposed to external competition, enterprises (and their workers) would have to become more efficient, competitive, and innovative if they were to survive. They would be forced to focus on research and development rather than rely on governments to do it for them. On a larger scale, the Australian economy would be "internationalized." The effect of these new economic policies, especially deregulation of financial markets and the floating of the Australian dollar (at the end of 1983), was to closely enmesh the Australian economy with the international economy and to reduce state autonomy in relation to economic decision-making. This reduced the Australian state's scope for action in relation to global fluctuations, and also resulted in the disciplining of the government by global market assessments (Bell and Head 1994: 18; Cox 1997).

Often, the supposed exigencies of "globalization" were trotted out to justify government decisions. For many governments at the state and national levels during the 1980s and 1990s, "globalization" (and before globalization became such a popular word, opening Australia up, modernizing Australia, and so on) became an ideology that could be brought out to justify political changes and policy shifts that were hurting many people (Beeson and Firth 1998; Conley 2001). Despite the fact that certain changes in the role of the state, and in the nature of the Australian economy were necessary, the actual response of governments in the 1980s and 1990s was not simply dictated by globalization, as many pundits claimed, but was a political response to globalization. Specific decisions made, such as the gradual winding down of arbitration and its replacement by enterprise bargaining and individual contracts; the extent of the deregulation of banking and capital flows; the speed and aggressiveness of tariff reductions, decisions on taxation (e.g., reducing corporate and higher personal income taxation); reductions in spending (especially on social welfare), and the decision to privatize and corporatize government services and utilities; were all political decisions among a range of choices.

Some Australians felt the reorientation of government in a very direct, economic way. Without high tariffs and other related forms of protection, some industries collapsed in the 1980s and 1990s, and people were thrown out of jobs, some of them, in particular semiskilled and unskilled blue collar workers, falling into long-term unemployment. Some social services were cut or reduced. Public service departments, at the Commonwealth and State levels, were downsized, streamlined, and transformed by new corporate management practices and structures, with some of their previous functions and activities outsourced to private enterprise, or opened up to competition ("compulsory competitive tendering" as it became known in Victoria during the 1990s). Hospitals, schools, rail lines, banks, post offices, and other services disappeared from many rural areas and suburbs of the cities in Australia in the 1980s and 1990s. While some regions prospered, others went backward (O'Connor et al. 2001), and because the state had reoriented itself, it ignored calls to redress such imbalances across Australia. Instead, people would have to retrain or relocate themselves to more prosperous regions. This was, many argued, the reality of living in a more internationally competitive nation and economy. People simply had to become more flexible and reflexive in the way that they approached the conduct of their own lives. The labor programs and job schemes, and the compensatory package for wage restraint — universal healthcare benefits through Medicare, expanded education, family payments, and so on — of the Labor governments of the 1980s and 1990s, negotiated with the trade unions under a series of Accords were ways of dealing with a high unemployment rate and the structural adjustments of the internationalized economy. These gave way to the mutual obligation and work-for-the-dole programs of the Liberal-National Howard government (1996–), which emphasized individual responsibility and hammered home the new reality that the state owed no one a living.

For those bruised by these changes, globalization was felt as the threat of the outside world, reducing all that they had valued about the country to the lowest common denominator. No longer, it seemed, was the state prepared to act as a neutral, relatively objective, third force in Australia, mediating, umpiring, and balancing the frictions, tensions, and conflicts between capital and labor, city and country. From the late 1980s onward, microeconomic reform began to focus on loosening Australia's traditionally centralized wage determination, amidst calls for enterprise bargaining and individual contracts that would allow the new entrepreneurial enterprises to compete in the world. Some commentators praised the fact that real wages were reduced during the 1980s and the first half of the 1990s, making Australian industry more competitive and attractive to local and overseas investment (Mitchell and Bassanese 2003). Given the historical development of Australian state–civil society relations — where the state was accepted as the avenue through which individuals would gain a decent living — it is no surprise that such massive changes resulted in feelings of vulnerability and disorientation among the populace. In other words, there were social implications of the state removing itself to let people get on with their lives.

Although some were cushioned, few could ignore the effects and the general social anxiety it produced (Little 1999; Mackay 1993).

None of this meant, in any simple way, the wholesale retreat of the state. The Australian state expanded its role in the 1980s as a facilitator of trade and export, establishing the Australian Trade Commission in 1986, searching out new markets in the Asia-Pacific region, developing a global marketing plan identifying the products most likely to find markets for export, and engaging in forums in pursuit of regional trade, economic, and institutional cooperation such as the Pacific Economic Cooperation Conference, the South Pacific Forum Secretariat (Meredith and Dyster 1999: 274), and Asia-Pacific Economic Cooperation (APEC), an institution initiated by the Hawke government in 1989 (Catley, 1996: chap. 9). The post-1970s Australian state has increasingly seen itself as a facilitator and regulator of the type that Held et al. (1999: 9) and Osborne and Gaebler (1992) call the catalytic state. It has embraced neoliberal principles, looked to the market to resolve economic, and some social problems, and has deregulated and abolished many of its former controls over banking, finance, commerce, and capital movements. At the same time, it has become increasingly regulatory in some areas like consumer protection, companies and securities regulation, and environmental protection (Bell and Head 1994: 20). It set up important statutory bodies like the Australian Competition and Consumer Commission (ACCC), concerned with policing fair competition. The state has maintained a concern with the ongoing development not only of the national economy but also of the national culture. Where once the Australian state was concerned with key nation-building policies in communication, transport, education, and health (including "racial" health), now it became the concern of government to push individuals and enterprises to be more open and risk-taking: to accept that this was the best way to get ahead in a globalizing world (Bryan and Rafferty 1999).

What is interesting in Australia's case is the way that efforts by the state to make Australia more competitive in the world economy, and the consequent changes to the state's way of functioning in Australia, have gone hand in hand with an emphasis on the national identity. From the renovation of an Australian identity under the post-1960s administrations of Whitlam (1972–1975), Fraser (1975–1983), Hawke (1983–1991), and Keating (1991–1996) (moving from a white Australian to a multicultural Australian identity), to the more recent defense of a traditional Australian identity by the administration of John Howard (1996–), Australia's political leaders have actively articulated national identity. In fact, the globalization of the Australian economy was itself conceived and articulated as a *national* project, not simply as an opening up of Australia to the world, and certainly not as a dissipation of Australian identity. Australian political leaders continue to speak in the language of a nation, as any examination of speeches, doorstop interviews, and explanation of policies attests. The major debates on necessary (and for some, unnecessary) changes of the last 20 years have all been national debates about the status and future of the Australian nation. There is, I think, even a case to be made for the way that the "nation" has become even more significant as a political object around which policy is shaped in this period of intensified globalization (Bryan and Rafferty 1999: chap. 4). This would be in accord with what some argue is the way globalization proceeds in the economic realm, with nation-states being the major players promoting it: in other words, globalization as the articulation of national interests (Hirst and Thompson 1999; Weiss 1998).

Why should this be so? One of the most important reasons is that the nation remains for the majority of the people, the most compelling form of political community, and focus for collective identity, even in this period of intensified globalization. There is no such thing as a world identity, let alone a world government that people of different nations could perceive as articulating their, always specific, interests. While transnational agreements and regulations proliferate, there are no transnational governments that, so far, rival the sovereignty and legitimacy of the governments of nations (Smith 1995). For Australian governments to maintain their legitimacy, they have to reinterpret the national story in the light of changed circumstances and new challenges. They cannot simply reinvent that story as they please, but must work with historically rooted memories, myths, and meanings (Smith 1993). An important feature of politics in Australia is the creative articulation of policy programs with conceptions of the national interest and identity.

One of the major aims of this book is to examine the different ways that Australian nationality has been reshaped in the period of intensified globalization, especially since the 1980s. The forces that contribute to this reshaping are varied. Many discussions of national identity under intensified globalization approach it from a level of rather abstract theorizing. I adopt a different approach, exploring everyday experiences of national identity in order to represent the diverse ways that Australians respond to globalization, and in particular, how they experience their national identity within that context.

As mentioned above, theorists have associated detradition-alization with globalization. Detraditionalization refers to the long-range process of rationalization and reflexivity associated with enlightenment or modernity: traditions become increasingly open to questioning, and people's actions and cultural modes become increasingly guided by discussion, debate, and the recourse to reasons rather than to legitimatization by what was done in the past, or by recourse to traditional authority. Paul Heelas defines the phenomenon in the following way:

> As a working definition, detraditionalization involves a shift of authority: from "without" to "within". It entails the decline of the belief in pre-given or natural orders of things. Individual subjects are themselves called upon to exercise authority in the face of the disorder and contingency which is thereby generated. 'Voice' is displaced from established sources, coming to rest with the self (1996: 2).

By opening up the flow of information and providing access to different forms of life, intensified globalization contributes to the process of detraditionalization, making it more difficult for those who would rely on traditional authority to sustain their claims. However, as Heelas and many others who write about globalization are well aware, the process is not as straightforward as that (see, e.g., Giddens 1999). There are obvious instances where tradition serves to legitimize social arrangements on a society-wide basis, as the examples of religious fundamentalism and the theocratic state prove. Traditions themselves can be dynamic, rather than simply the dead weight of the past. Globalization does not mean simply the disappearance of traditions but also the reinvention of traditions, the clash of traditions, and the emergence of the new. Australia's political and cultural traditions, both indigenous and nonindigenous, have not been swept aside by the tide of globalization. But they have been questioned, threatened, reinvented, and sometimes overturned as Australia launched itself into the twenty-first century.

It is perhaps more obvious in the context of a discussion of detraditionalization to examine the impact of globalization (understood here as different phases of colonization) on "traditional" indigenous cultures. I explore the complexities of this situation in Chapter Four, where I show that it is not simply a case of the overcoming and dismantling of indigenous tradition, but one of the reappropriation and continuity of tradition by and among indigenous communities, even in the context of the "multivocal complexities of our times" (Heelas 1996: 3). There is, however, another way to think about tradition: how time-honored ways of doing things are affected by globalization, and how such ways of doing things interact with globalization. In this respect, one can think of political traditions.

Social scientists used to talk about national character and, flowing on from this, about national political cultures (Inkeles and Levinson 1969; Pye 1968). The assumption was that a country's unique historical experiences gave rise to a distinctive political culture, and that people could be expected to behave in certain general ways in accordance with that culture. Social scientists developed increasingly intricate survey methods to categorize different political cultures around the world.

In its classic definitions, political culture was understood as the broad pattern of beliefs, attitudes, orientations, sentiments, and feelings supporting the political system and its institutions. It was concerned with the relationship between the individual personality (or psychology) and the broader cultural framework, mediated by processes of socialization. It involved things like characteristic attitudes and orientations to authority and power; understandings of the political process; levels of trust in politicians and the political system; notions of the limits of politics; the division between the public and the private realm; and so on. As the concept developed, it came to include the people's sense of national identity, its sense of national belonging (the dominant style, or styles, of its national imagining), and its understanding of the nature and basis of its political community (Almond and Verba 1963; Almond 1989). In the hands of some, like Lucian Pye (1968), the concept was supple: it took into consideration the political subcultures that existed within states, not only as evident in the orientations and attitudes of the political elite as opposed to the masses, but within the subcultures of the masses, where competing forms could coexist based on class, ethnic, or other associations and identifications. Political culture, as a broad umbrella encompassing these various subcultures, was thus also concerned with the pattern of relationships between subcultures.

The assumption underpinning such approaches was the relative boundedness of the nation-state and of the national community, something that many globalization theorists argue is becoming less of a reality in today's world. To speak of a distinct Australian political culture — or for that matter, of an Australian national identity — in an age of intensified globalization might be controversial in the view of some of these theorists. In an age where boundaries have become more permeable, and identities more fluid and uncertain, the notion of political culture might appear as a relic of a more stable past. However, even under the impact of global forces, social experience is not simply about change and flow, but involves boundaries (including national ones), structuring, shared feelings, beliefs, orientations and attitudes, and struggles for identity.

Australian political culture developed over time and through historical experience. It would be a mistake to think of it, or any political culture for that matter, as formed in the past and then remaining the same throughout a nation's development. Political culture is more dynamic than that. It is at once shaped by historical experience, and gives shape to historical experience. It is the means through and by which people negotiate and adapt to political and social change (Capling et al. 1998). Global processes shaped it in the past, and the increased interconnectedness of the globe shapes and transforms it in the present.

Most accounts of Australian political culture begin by stressing the strong support of Australians for an interventionist state. I have already discussed this, citing its historical context. One might legitimately wonder how that old style interventionist state has been so comprehensively dismantled and refashioned since the 1980s if it was so central to the political culture. The point here, I think, is to see political culture as complex and dynamic, not simply as a force resistant to change. There were always competing views of the correct role of the state, even during that long period of political consensus between the major parties on what the state should do, how much it should spend, and so on. In any case, Australians had little choice but to accept such transformation, as it was largely carried through under a bipartisan agreement between Australia's major political parties, each under the sway of neoliberal ideology. When they were offered the opportunity of electing a Liberal–National government even more committed to neoliberal economic ideals, Paul Keating won the "unwinnable" election in 1993 by committing his next Labor government to a more "compassionate" society. Opposition leader John Hewson, a former economist, had promised to slash spending on social welfare and to dismantle Australia's industrial relations system, detailed in his *Fightback!* Package (Brett 2003; Watson 2002). Furthermore, there is evidence enough in reactions to such a transformation to suggest the existence of certain salient expectations about what the state should do, among the Australian populace (Conley 2001 cites some of the evidence; see also Pusey 2003).

Opinion polling suggests that a majority of Australians support limiting the import of foreign products in order to protect the national economy and that, at least to this extent, they oppose free trade and an open global economy (Evans and Kelley 2002: 221–227). There has been a notable lack of enthusiasm among the general public for the series of privatizations of government services and utilities undertaken by governments at the state and national levels during the 1990s. There is no doubt that Australians, based on their historical experience, are committed to notions of public ownership in some areas of social life. A recent national poll found the following percentages of respondents "agreeing that governments should wholly or mainly own selected services": prisons 76 percent, public transport 50 percent, water 71 percent, electricity 59 percent, gas 50 percent, telephones 36 percent, and hospitals 60 percent. Taking the question around the other way — "respondents agreeing that the private sector should wholly or mainly own selected service" — the percentages are as follows: prisons 2 percent, public transport 12 percent, water 9 percent, electricity 14 percent, gas 19 percent, telephones 22 percent, and hospitals 7 percent. Respondents were generally lukewarm about "public/private partnerships in selected services," with the following percentages in favor: prisons 19 percent, public transport 34 percent, water 17 percent, electricity 25 percent, gas 27 percent, telephones 38 percent, and hospitals 35 percent (Hayward 2002: 10). As the author of the survey comments, citing other opinion polls, this ongoing support for public ownership had held throughout the 1990s, despite government enthusiasm for privatization. Although the Howard government sold off almost half of Australia's main telecommunications company Telstra, a majority of the population has continued to oppose the selling off of the remainder. One of our respondents, Neil (quoted earlier), expressed some of the doubts others, especially those living in rural and regional areas, might have felt when I asked him about the impact of privatization:

> I think that's brought a lot of fear into the community, even amongst people who are free enterprizers. They believe that big business can't be trusted. If they analyzed their thinking that's what that'd be … . People want to see the essential services in government hands. (*Like electricity, gas, water?*) And telephone and even the railways. Yes. Because there's a fear of being taken over by big companies. I mean they even talk about [the fact that] there's French money in some of these investments in Australia. (*What do you think that fear is about?*) It's that, well, they won't be there for the people's benefit. The culture of Australians is that we might be free enterprise people but we need these facilities to feed our industries or to feed our wants and knowing that their charter is for the good of the community. (*Of Australia?*) Of Australia yeah.

This statist tradition was linked to, and often served, a second political tradition: economic nationalism. Indeed, notions of public ownership and state intervention in the economy, and the drive to develop Australia's manufacturing base can be explained, at least in part, by Australians' concern to establish national autonomy and self-sufficiency, based on their experiences of a sometimes hostile international environment. Capling et al. argue, for example, that Australians were determined that they would not again be caught out by the interruption to the flow of required goods that they experienced during the First World War. Nor would they be exposed to the social devastation of Depression and unemployment. The first stirrings of economic nationalism can be found even earlier, they point out, in prefederation days when the colony of Victoria first introduced tariff barriers (1999: chap. 2). Although the generations shaped by the Depression are being replaced by generations not directly touched by such privations, economic nationalism remains a powerful trend in Australian political culture.

A third important feature of Australian political culture, according to most accounts, is its egalitarianism (Thompson 1994). This is both celebrated as the national ethos, and critiqued by some as "leveling" or, as it is referred to in Australia, the "tall poppy syndrome." Russel Ward in his famous book *The Australian Legend* (1966) saw this egalitarianism as emerging from the early formative experiences of the "nomad tribe" of rural "pastoral" workers, many of them convicts and ex-convicts, who defied authority, and by material necessity and due to other forces such as colonial oppression, climate, and the rigors of outback life and work on the large pastoral runs, experienced a powerful sense of solidarity, a disdain for airs and graces, and the belief that every man was equal. This ethos spread upward through the society as it developed and became more organized. Egalitarianism does not entail that there are no social or class divisions, there always have been, but that Australians think of themselves as equals, and expect to be treated that way. Australia is, as John Hirst (2002: chap. 10) has recently argued, a "democracy of manners." The rules of deference characteristic of the "home country" (Britain) and of other European class societies (the Old World) would have no place in Australia (Horne 1964; Hughes 1973). Don, a semi-retired doctor who I will discuss in more detail in the next chapter, when asked to describe the Australia he had known during the course of his long life, said that "what was distinctive about it was its egalitarian nature, its sense of equality and social justice and the fact that at various times it was prepared to go to pretty great lengths to preserve those characteristics." Related to this egalitarianism is the very Australian notion of the "fair go," a phrase that's importance to the Australian ethos is evident in the way that it is so quickly picked up and emphasized by immigrants. The "fair go" means that everyone in Australia should be given a fair chance in life, and a fair hearing.

This broad egalitarian tradition in combination with Australians' acceptance of a strong interventionist role for the state meant that Australians looked to the government to smooth out the inequalities endemic to a competitive, capitalist market economy, through government support in the areas of education, health, and other policies of redistribution and, in the latter half of the twentieth century, through progressive taxation. Although Australians accept that there should be a distribution of incomes based on education, skill, merit and effort, and favor equality of opportunity rather than equality of outcome, compared with other OECD countries, Australians favor lower levels of income inequality in their society (Evans and Kelley 2002: 209–220; Kelley et al. 1996; for an overview of polling on income inequality issues, albeit one that points to various anomalies in Australian attitudes, see Smith 2001: chap. 5). But this is exactly what globalization has brought in its wake to Australia, just as it has in other places. The opening up of the economy, technological change, the reorientation of state activity, and the tightening and streamlining of state spending in welfare and other areas, have had an important impact on equality of incomes, contributing to a widening gap between the rich and the poor in Australia. Not only have these changes contributed to insecurity and poverty among the lower income workforce who experience increasing levels of casualization of their labor (Borland et al. 2001) but they have also stimulated a sense of nervousness, and even resentment among those "middle Australians" who have not gone under but who feel the burden of competitiveness and flexibility (Pusey 2003).

A fourth important feature of Australian political culture, and closely intertwined with the other features, is its democratic nature. Australia has had more than 150 years of democratic government. When the colonies of South Australia, New South Wales, Victoria, and Tasmania achieved self-government in the 1850s, manhood suffrage soon followed in all except Tasmania, which achieved it in 1900. South Australia pioneered the secret ballot in 1856 (Costar 1997: 226). Women got the vote in several colonies in the last decade of the nineteenth century (pioneered again by South Australia in 1894), and were granted it at the Commonwealth level soon after federation, through the 1902 *Commonwealth Franchise Act*. With the notable exception of

Aborigines (who were disenfranchised by the same 1902 Act), most adults at both state and federal levels had the vote in the early twentieth century. Australia's robust democratic institutions are supported by robust democratic impulses among its citizens (Hirst 2002). Globalization, including pressures on the state to open economic flows and to reduce spending, have, as in other democratic states, reduced the role of the state in shaping Australian society. There is evidence that a majority of Australians feel that the government should be doing more to solve things like unemployment and to provide major social services, especially in the areas of health and education (Pusey 2003). Antiglobalization protesters, from many walks of life, call for a greater democratic control of the activities of multinational companies.

A fifth feature of the political culture is what Capling et al. (1998) call the "independence ideal" — broadly, that each member of society should stand on his or her own two feet, and be proud to be independent. This was the promise that Australia held out to many settlers in the nineteenth century, giving rise to pioneering myths and related myths of the independent yeoman farmer. This might appear to contradict the belief and faith in interventionist government, but only if one holds that the government is perceived as paternal and protective, rather than as the collective means to ensure conditions conducive to independence. As Hancock (1930) argued, individuals viewed the state as a "vast public utility" to further their individual ends. The independence ideal has been expressed historically in different ways, from the independence of labor supported by worker solidarity and the "living wage" (the independent worker able to support his family without aid from the state or charity), to the independent farmer or businessman. It finds expression in the high value placed by Australians on home ownership, and in the generally high rates of home ownership characteristic in Australia since the late nineteenth century. It is tied with notions of citizenship and moral worth (Brett 1992, 2003). The independence ideal also helps explain why Australians have traditionally disapproved of unemployment benefits except in cases of proven need, and are against greater government expenditure on the unemployed (Smith 2001: 117–121). Instead of welfare, they want work.

As with egalitarianism, the independence ideal is threatened for many by rising insecurity, the casualization of jobs, and the consequent loss of entitlements such as sickness and holiday pay in the new globalized economy. These changes make it difficult for many people to make long-term financial and other plans. Caught in the pincer movement of uncertain employment and escalating house prices, a significant section of Australians is being excluded from the housing market. There are many other ways in which the ideal of independence is being undermined by the new conditions of globalization. On the other hand, the independence ideal is being reinvented as hyperindividualism and the expansion of consumer choice, including areas like health and social welfare previously cordoned off from such logics. In the late 1990s, when the Howard government replaced the Commonwealth Employment Service with a privatized Job Network system, it claimed that this would provide individual unemployed "consumers" with a better range of choices to suit their specific needs.

Finally, no account of the dominant strains within Australian political culture would be complete without considering the centrality of assimilationist ideas and desires.

What unified the society and the nation, according to this ideology, was a common way of life, shared beliefs, attitudes, ideals, and values, rooted in a common racial belonging (white Australia). This meant that, even when the racial understanding of national unity lost legitimacy after the Second World War, Australians, publicly and privately, argued the case for a common way of life for the whole of society. There would, and should, be no ethnic or other enclaves of difference within a united Australian society. Australian egalitarianism has largely been of this assimilationist variety.

This assimilationist strand of Australian political culture has been thoroughly questioned under conditions of intensified globalization. The character of the national community changed substantially during the twentieth century, and globalizing processes made important contributions to these changes. Despite its important political, religious, and class divisions, there is no doubt that until the end of the Second World War Australia was a relatively homogenous society. In the 1930s, commentators like Hancock (1930) noted the way in which the same manner of life was observed from one end of the country to the other: the same kinds of dwellings, the same manner and type of household expenditure, the same kinds of food, the same Christian values, and so on (see also Eggleston 1953). This is no longer the case. Australia is now far more socially, culturally, religiously, and ethnically diverse (for a statistical summary, see National Multicultural Advisory Council 1999: Statistical Appendix). It is in the process of becoming a polyethnic nation, and its identities are becoming more cosmopolitan, especially in the major cities. The new ethnic diversity of the Australian population is the outcome of the immigration program after the Second World War, and the move to nondiscriminatory immigration after the White Australia Policy was incrementally abandoned from the mid 1950s. I explore the complex implications of these developments in Chapter Three. To this diversity, we can add the emergence of new forms of gay and lesbian identities (Altman 2001), and various youth and other subcultures.

Progressive changes in relations between the settler and indigenous populations since the 1970s, but especially since the 1990s, have also contributed to this new diversity of identities, or in the case of indigenous peoples, to the increased public visibility of their identities. While the assimilationist policy framework has been partially dismantled since the 1970s, and governments have explicitly embraced what they call policies of integration, self-determination, self-management, and reconciliation in place of assimilation, the cultural embeddedness of assimilationist thinking remains among politicians and the public. National surveys, and nationwide focus group studies, for example, continue to reveal the expectation that indigenous people should aspire to be more like the rest of the Australian population (Irving Saulwick and Associates 2000; Newspoll Market Research 2000).

Australia developed a distinctive political culture in the course of more than 150 years of democratic government and social experimentation. This influences Australians' negotiation of globalization today: the reception of globalization discourses, the acceptance of changes to the role of the state, views about what politicians should and should not do (the limits of politics), and the particular inflections of anxiety about where globalization is taking them and their nation. As Capling et al. (1998) point out, however, globalization, and in particular economic liberalization, is contributing to transforming this political culture in significant ways. The political culture, they say, "is in the midst of transformative turbulence" (Capling et al. 1998: 133). In the remaining chapters of this book, I will investigate some of this turbulence.

Kel had been a shearer in his earlier days. Now in his late forties, he still keeps himself busy, running a few sheep on a bit of land he owned, while making money by organizing the sale of cattle in town. He had lived in and traveled through many parts of Australia, and liked much of what he had seen — the people, the places, the landscape. He had never been overseas. When he woke up each morning and looked out the window he still thought Australia "was the best country in the world." I asked him whether he thought it was important to have an Australian identity:

Oh yeah, for sure. When my kids were little I actually taught them Australian poems by Banjo Patterson and C.J. Dennis and things like that ... Henry Lawson ... because I think those people gave a picture of what Australia was like back in the early days ... . I think that's where we're losing our identity because it's more global now. Everyone's the same. You can walk down the street in New York. A friend of mine's just come back from over in New York, a girlfriend of mine and she showed me all the photos. I would say that you'd think that you were walking down the main street of this [regional] town. You've got Maccas and all those sorts of things there. It just seems to be the same. The supermarkets are taking over and we're losing our corner stores. Like the old lady down the corner store, she used to be the hub of the town once because she knew all the news. It's like the post office. The bloke in the post office used to know all the people who lived in the town and things like that. But now it just seems to be losing our, oh I don't know what the word means, but you're just becoming too global.

Kel lived outside the regional town where we met. Later, he assured me that there were still plenty of "country" people with a real Australian identity out in the backblocks:

You travel out in the back country or out in the farming communities, they think and do a lot different to what people do in the city. People in the country are staying more with the Australian culture side of things, whereas people in the city are becoming more Americanized. I think that's going to be a big division in years to come.

Cities, according to some theorists, are the engine rooms of globalization (Sassen 1998). Globalization has meant the emergence of global cities like New York, Tokyo, London, and Paris. Occasionally, Sydney makes it onto those lists, or at least onto the B-grade lists. Australians frequently comment on the difference between the city and the country when it comes to national character or identity. Australian cities are seen as far more cosmopolitan, far more multicultural, and less distinctively Australian than rural and regional areas. Some still go in search of the "real" Australia in the bush. What they find, however, might be quite different from what they had imagined. Globalization is having its impact there too (Gray and Lawrence 2001), from privatization of services and the deregulation of agricultural industries contributing to high levels of dislocation, unemployment, and for some, personal alienation, to the use of rural towns as places of settlement for refugees and other new immigrants. Being a local in rural and regional Australia has a different meaning from what it had even twenty years ago. The transformation of telecommunications, access to the Internet, international and national television and radio have meant, for example, that there is a level of continuity between the youth cultures of cities and country areas, linked up with international youth cultures, that was less the case in the past. Although the older generations may have been less affected by this communication revolution in a cultural sense, they have not been immune to its effects, like the ways that it has brought the outside world into their local environments, reshaping them in the process (Giddens 1990). Moreover, global problems such as drug abuse epidemics are no longer restricted to the city, but now penetrate the Australian countryside.

Despite being one of the most urbanized nations in the world, there remains a cultural tendency among Australians to see the "real Australia" as emanating from, and residing in, the bush rather than the cities (Kapferer 1990), a phenomenon noted decades ago by influential social commentators like Donald Horne (1964). Mick, the Vietnam veteran quoted in the last chapter, when he was first interviewed in the late 1980s, and at that time living in a major city, spoke passionately about the national virtues to be found in the bush. By contrast, living in cities you could be anywhere in the world, he explained. He yearned to live where the community was on a smaller scale and where the old Australian values of mateship, friendliness, and taking things in your stride, still prevailed, where he could meet and live among "old Australian types." When Mick was interviewed again recently, he had followed his dream of moving to a country homestead on several acres of land. The scenes that confronted him every day were, undoubtedly, very Australian, with the views from his veranda overlooking a valley and bushland. On the other hand, he was shocked at what he saw of the social breakdown and the sense of hopelessness in the rural towns. Some people lived in dire poverty, there was simply nothing for young people to do, unemployment was high, and drug abuse seemed to touch everybody's lives. Railway stations were unattended and run-down, and health and transport services were in decline. As mentioned in the previous chapter, the livelihood of the surrounding towns was threatened by the rise of transnational companies replacing local companies.

Mick battled to maintain a sense of Australianness amidst all of this change. While people in the cities had become indistinguishable "world people" in his eyes, he still felt that people were more Australian where he now lived. He was passionate about the "old," "true blue" Australian type he associated with the working class, bushworkers, and Australian servicemen. To serve the country in war, as he had done, he experienced as a sacred duty, and doing so gave him a certain spiritual experience of nationhood. It was clear that for Mick, it was still vitally important to have an Australian identity.

The virtues of the bush and its people can be, however, read as the opposite: as small mindedness and overfamiliarity, leading to boredom and a stultifying life. The move from the country to the city can be experienced as a widening of horizons and a loosening up of identity, even as the throwing off of an older Australianness.

Cheryl, a young executive in a large company, had moved as a teenager from her country farm, where she had been surrounded by people who "were sort of similar in a sense," to the city where people and lifestyles were more diverse. Since coming to the city, her attitude and lifestyle had become increasingly cosmopolitan, to the extent that she no longer felt particularly Australian. She now had many Russian Jewish and European (especially Italian) friends and she closely identified with them and with what she knew of their culture. Such friends had given her, she felt, a greater exposure to emotion, and to expressing emotion and accepting emotional display than she had encountered growing up in a predominantly Anglo-Celtic rural community. Simply being around these more "worldly" and outward-looking people, who had a more "realistic" understanding of Australia's place among nations, had given her a broader perspective on the world. "When in the country," she reflected, "I didn't have any exposure to those sorts of people."

Working for a large, transnational company of Australian origin also gave Cheryl an orientation to the world, which meant that her horizons expanded beyond Australia. She was interested in the ways in which other countries and cultures worked. This had a practical dimension — if the company was going to make real inroads into Japan, for example, then people had to learn to understand and appreciate in a deep sense the way in which Japanese society worked. But Cheryl also felt an emotional pull to be involved with other cultures:

Whenever I've traveled I've not been a "going and seeing the sights" person. We went to India for four weeks, and actually spent it in one small area, really getting involved in village life, and to me it's to try and get an understanding of the whole culture and the whole way people think within that organization. It's really trying I suppose to get an understanding of what

being an Indian is all about, rather than looking at it in terms of
monuments or whatever, understanding the political system.

Travel had lifted her out of her older Australian identity, and
she had even contemplated moving to another part of the
world. Australia did not look like the place it once was. In a
sense, once she had left her childhood home and once her parents had passed away, home was wherever she chose it to be.
Whether this was, in part, a fantasy that would not withstand
the actual experience of living and working outside Australia
is beside the point. The real point is that Cheryl's experience of
work and the world threw her national identity into question,
or at the very least relegated it to a less prominent position in
the hierarchy of her identity.

Ulf Hannerz (1996), reflecting on Robert Reich's *The Work of
Nations* (1991), has argued that there are some people within
modern nation-states for whom there has been a "weakening
of the nation as imagined community and source of identity"
(1996: 81). The nature of the work and transnational connections of these people, linked as they are "to global webs of
enterprise," tend to lift them out of the nation. Those working
in the "symbolic-analytic services," "research scientists, various
kinds of engineers, investment bankers, lawyers ..., consultants, corporate headhunters, publishers and writers, musicians,
television and film producers," academics, and so on, although
they live within nations in a physical sense, are less imaginatively engaged in the national community. "Among the tribes
of symbolic analysts," he writes, "we seem to get a close-up
view of the nation retreating ... . They build their own monuments — like the convention centers, the research parks, the
international airports — and withdraw into their own private

habitats, enclaves with security guards if need be" (1996: 84). These people are footloose, as it were, less tied to national economies even as they engage in obligatory and routine acts of nationalist recognition. They are less connected to, or reliant upon, the economic performance of other social categories within the national space. Their skills and forms of knowledge are transferrable and translatable, and not dependent upon particular places and organizations.

In its best guise, nationalism and a strong sense of belonging to a national community, can provide support for larger schemes of social betterment that individuals might not perceive as directly benefiting their own lives. The welfare state draws its support from the willingness of the different classes in Australian society to contribute to a set of institutions and benefits that would lead to the improvement and welfare of the society as a whole. Because of shared national identity, and a sense of belonging to a common political community, people feel a sense of obligation to others within that community. The argument has been developed by writers like David Miller (1993, 1995), in his defense of nationality: we are prepared to accept certain government programs for our national compatriots; but we may not feel that such measures should be extended beyond the boundaries of the nation-state. We have a special ethical commitment to others within the national boundary.

One of the potential problems of a weakening of the sense of national belonging, especially among the wealthier professional class, is the way in which this might contribute to a weakening sense of obligation to others in the national community. Thus, the popularity of tax concessions for the wealthy, or for those with higher incomes, has contributed to the weakening financial basis for the welfare state in Australia, as it has in other western countries. One might feel, as Hannerz points out, more of a connection with people in one's own profession or field in other countries, and even a sense of solidarity with them and their concerns, than with conationals, whose lives are completely alien and divorced from one's own. On the other hand, one wonders to what extent such forms of imaginative separation from the national community are luxuries that people can only afford when everything is going well. When jobs are lost or become precarious, or the social conditions where one predominantly lives — and most of us still live in nations most of the time — become more hazardous, whether it be through natural disaster, economic crisis, political instability, or terrorist threat — then the feeling of nationness can reassert itself powerfully. Most recently, in Australia, such surges of national feeling were palpable at the time of the Bali bombings, and even in the context of the bushfires that raged in the southeastern states in the summer of 2002 to 2003. If it is true, as Anderson (1983: 17–19) suggests, that nationalism has been so successful as an ideology because it attends to feelings of vulnerability and mortality, then one might expect that nationalism, and feelings of belonging to national community might become more intense when one experiences personal adversity.

Tjaart's reflections on the course of his life provide a salutary example in this respect, charting an early flirtation with the pleasures and promises of globalization, to the realization that his life was, after all, much more local and national than he had earlier imagined. From a Dutch immigrant family, Tjaart was an entrepreneur in his mid-thirties when he was first interviewed in the 1980s. He was a successful self-made businessman, whose company in an emerging service industry rapidly expanded during the 1980s. In other words, he did extremely well from the opening up of the Australian economy.

At that time, Tjaart was unabashed and even celebratory in embracing private interest at the expense of notions of national solidarity or commitment to those less fortunate. Tjaart's ideal society was one where individuals were free to sink or swim depending on their efforts, natural abilities, and commitment to work. He was annoyed that his taxes were being redirected to the poor. In his view, this meant taking from the productive and enterprising middle class, with which he strongly identified, to give to the lower and less enterprising classes. The deregulation of finance had given him a new lever for pressuring government. Toward the end of the 1980s, he was thinking of relocating his business, or sections of it, overseas, in order to avoid the Australian taxation regime. His perspective was global. He looked to countries like Singapore that he felt had a more business-friendly environment. His view on the poor was that it should be left to the charities to look after them. Government should step back:

> In my view of things, there's always going to be someone who's in the poor bracket or who's described as being poor... . And the same with really sad cases of hardships and all those sorts of things. There will always be those people so I tend not to be overly concerned, or that is not a high priority trying to, you know, make sure that everybody has a feed. You can keep on going and everybody else can keep on working towards that, I'd much rather do what I do, okay?

Hierarchy, he argued, was the natural structure of a society. He envisioned and desired an enterprise society where businesses like his own would be given their head, and where those who did not have the drive to set up their own, or to work hard within the enterprises set up by others, would be left behind. He felt no obligation to them.

When interviewed again in 2002, Tjaart's attitudes had mellowed considerably. Having faced financial ruin himself during the 1990s, he could see the downside to the intense competition of Australia's globalized economy. He also realized that his type of business was not the kind that could be easily transported and set up elsewhere, and that his success in fact depended on locality and on the long-term building of relations of trust with steady clients. He spoke of the importance of the business name, of ethics and of loyalty. He had been buffeted by a much harsher economic environment where larger businesses had been able to undercut him, and where he had felt the direct impact of the communications revolution. He sensed a decline of an older kind of citizenship, and the rise of rights over responsibilities, although he had no social explanation for this. Referring to the rise of social helplessness and alienation, of poverty and homelessness that tended to be hidden away, he lamented "It's a little bit sickening I suppose, the society that we have."

One of the most important changes in his life was getting married and taking on the shared responsibility of raising his wife's children from a previous marriage. This not only made him less footloose, and much more committed to the place where he lived and worked, but it gave him a new perspective on the difficult circumstances of youth in the modern, open Australia with its overwhelming number of choices, possibilities, and uncertainties.

Life experiences, one might say, drew Tjaart back into the nation after a brief flirtation with being a global player. He came to accept what he perhaps always knew: that his life was rooted in a particular locale, with particular people (family, friends, employees, and business associates), his own destiny bound up with the trials and tribulations of the Australian nation and economy, buffeted as it was by global competition.

National identity has had different formative contexts in Australia. One way to think about this is in terms of generations. One can trace the formation of what has been an important and characteristic experience of national identity in Australia by listening to the account that Don, a successful, semiretired rural general practitioner, gave of his life when interviewed at the end of the 1980s. Throughout his life, Don had been committed to public ideals and to serving the Australian nation. In fact, such a sense of service was second nature to Don. He had been a direct participant in the expansion of the social welfare state in the postwar period, holding senior positions in city and rural public hospitals. Apart from his professional role, he had been actively involved in local community life through committees, clubs, associations, and charities. For some time in the 1960s, he recalled fondly, he and his wife were involved in "every bloody bunfight going on in town." He was well-connected, having experienced central and powerful positions within important national institutions during the course of his life. He was gentlemanly and polite, with a strong egalitarian streak and a commitment to social justice and to the ideals of nation-building characteristic of the 1950s and 1960s in Australia.

Despite the distinguishing features of what had been a remarkable life, Don's story is also representative of a certain generational experience of life in Australia. Australian social researcher Hugh Mackay (1997: chap. 2) calls Don's generation "the Lucky Generation": people of this generation often described themselves as "lucky" despite witnessing the Depression and living through, some of them fighting in, the Second World War. They ascribed their luck to "timing," to being born into a generational cycle that experienced high levels of security and economic well-being during their adult years, but with the valuable lessons of privation against which to measure these experiences. "In the Lucky generation's reflections on 'the lessons of childhood,'" Mackay writes, "five themes recur: loyalty, saving, the work ethic, the sense of mutual obligation, and patriotism" (1997: 17).

Born in the early 1920s, Don lived through the upheaval of the Depression and the Second World War, and adopted a belief in solidarity and national community from those experiences. He reached adulthood during the Second World War, where he was badly wounded on the Kokoda Trail. There, he experienced a profound act of human solidarity when he was saved, and carried out of the jungle, by Papua New Guineans. As he stressed, they were complete strangers, he was completely at their mercy, and to that day he wondered what motivated them to perform such an altruistic act. War did not simply provide him with that experience of human solidarity: it also cemented his sense of Australian solidarity. People looked after each other there, and engaged in acts of great selflessness and self-sacrifice. His ideal society would, he said, involve the honesty, straightforwardness, and comradeship he found on the Kokoda Trail — but without the war or aggression. Such a society would be based on the ideal of love of one's fellow men, which Don felt intensely.

Don's national identity was forged in a much smaller prewar society, a more homogenous, locally based and cohesive Australia. Things were less complicated in the past in Don's view.

He described an idyllic childhood spent in a historic mining town, with guiding parents keen on education and who closely watched over their sons' future prospects. Generalizing beyond the personal, Don saw that this was a time when fathers laid out life-plans for their sons, and when sons, feeling a sense of duty and knowing that there was no other or better way of going about things, did not resist. You knew that you had to obey your parents; but you had complete faith that they had your best interests at heart. Don spoke of the comfort of that past when things were only "black and white," as he put it. Clear gender patterns, a clear division of labor and of human traits, were part of this. He described the house where he grew up as secure and ordinary, part of a uniform pattern of houses, framing a close-knit community of achievers and strivers, surrounded by relatives and friends, and where home was the center of social life. He liked the way in which the house seemed to fit with the whole pattern of his life. The mood there was "fantastic" — directed, stimulating, a hive of purposeful activity.

Part of what Don liked about his early formative years was the way that his environment allowed him to know exactly where he was going, and to be free of the distractions of the outside world. Young people could plan for life once they knew what their role would be. They were also free of the tyranny of choice and open-endedness. They were also free of envy, as everyone around them had a similar life-pattern:

> We didn't know, you see, communications, we'd have radios or might've had a radio later on, but you didn't know, you never really knew that there was any other type of existence other than the one you were leading at the time. So there was never envy or this sort of business.

Don, like others of his generation, referred to the corrosive impact of television and materialism — Neil, the retired farmer and unionist quoted in the last chapter, emphasized the same thing. Don was free of envy, not only because everyone around him seemed to be living the same kind of life but also because he and those around him were simply not aware of the range of choices people now have in contemporary Australian society. Television had changed all of that, and affluence had unleashed new desires. By the same token, the national culture was more homogenous when he was younger, at least from this viewpoint, because it simply did not have the range of influences, the examples of different lifestyles, available to people today.

Don's sense of nationality, although forged through hard experience, was not something particularly open to reflection. It simply *was*, and gave rise to a certain sense of duty toward his fellow nationals. He admitted to feeling a powerful sense of national pride, especially when he thought about the way that Australia and Australians had survived through adversity. One of Don's guiding beliefs was that adversity and difficult beginnings can breed character and solidarity. This is the way it was for individuals — and he had his own experiences to draw upon — and that is the way it was for larger collectivities like nations. Describing Australia, Don said that "the main thing I would emphasize is that this nation started in travail and succeeded in travail and prospered by travail and now, reluctantly, I'd say that the nation's kind of lost that urge." I will return to this last point in a moment.

Don's national identity was rooted in a strong generational identification going back to his grandfather, who had been a political figure involved in the formation of the Australian

Labor Party. His father imbued him with a strong sense of history, beginning with visits as a boy to the important historic sites of the mining town where much of his family's history was embedded. He also imbued Don with the sense of the virtue of public service: he had been a committed, dedicated teacher for his entire working life, admired by his pupils and colleagues, never advancing up the public education department's hierarchy, putting his own personal ambitions aside.

Don viewed Australia as a national community where the bonds between people mattered, and where you had to care about what happened to everyone else since you were all in it together. In his view of Australian life, everyone should have a role, and all such roles were necessary for the proper functioning of a just and humane society. (At one point, Don retells Anatole France's fable "Our Lady's Juggler," where the moral is that everyone should do their particular job to the best of their ability, as each job is equally worthwhile in the eyes of the Lord.) Indeed, while recognizing that people would occupy different positions that would bring different levels of status, prestige, and material benefit, he was committed to the kind of deep horizontal solidarity ("comradeship") that Anderson (1983) says is characteristic of the nation as an imagined community.

Public space had a strong resonance for Don. The public world was where he could express himself, meet interesting people, and find out new things, and it was valued as such. It was also where he experienced solidarity. Humans, as he said, were "herd" animals; they needed group life to survive and prosper.

While Don felt a strong sense of belonging to a national civil society in which he had a role and a place, he suspected, from the vantage point of the 1980s, that this society was getting away from him. He yearned for a more stable time in the past when things were more in place and dependable, when you could know today what things would be like tomorrow.

As I have been suggesting, in Don's story we see one important version of the modern national self: purposeful, consistent, bounded by family, and by local and national community. In his depiction, there is a sense of continuity between his father's life and his own. When comparing their lives, he felt that their characters and the shape of their lives had been pretty much the same, only that they had lived through different historical circumstances, and had different opportunities. That self was morally secure — Don had always known where he was going, and what his duty was. But we can also sense Don's bewilderment at the changing life around him. It was noticeable that his description of the relationship he had with his father was strikingly different from his relationship with his two sons, who had struck out on their own, and whose lives he could not really understand.

For Don, Australia's high point came in the postwar period, a time of cohesion and nation-building. War had been a pivotal experience, and stimulated a brief national flowering. People were committed to rehabilitating the country, and experienced a high sense of morale. They worked together for a cause, and knew exactly why they were doing it, just like in the army at war. Australia had triumphed through adversity, struggle, and hard work, but now after peaking in the 1960s, it was in a state of decline. When trying to think of what lay behind this decline, Don described Australia as becoming too materialistic. Where once Australia had been a virile young nation making a lot out of nothing in a short space of time, now Australians had lost their work ethic, and lost their moral direction. Too many people were just working for money, and there was too little commitment to the larger community beyond the self. Australia was becoming the "white trash of the Pacific."

The entrepreneurial eighties had, in Don's view, shifted Australian decency off the map. Australians began to "worship Mammon," and they lost their commitment to egalitarianism and social justice. This was evident in the way that doctors went on strike in an effort to gain better pay, in the way that businessmen criticized taxation and invented schemes of tax evasion, and in widespread attacks on the welfare state. He used the analogy of sporting stars changing teams to illustrate the corrosive effects of money, materialism and the loss of identity, solidarity, and commitment. He felt saddened that local loyalties were increasingly lost. In his image of the past, life was rooted in a locale, where one's loyalty and identity lay, and this was a building block for larger identities, like nationality. He did not blame individuals themselves — who could blame a footballer changing teams for money, given the prevailing incentives and dog-eat-dog climate? But rather the way that money and the desires unleashed by affluence led to the breakdown of older certainties. Money was becoming more important than loyalty to place. Australians now placed money-makers on a pedestal, whereas if there was to be any legitimate status hierarchy in Australia, those placed at the top should be those who truly contributed to society: through personal sacrifice, through public service, through expanding the cultural life, or through scientific and artistic endeavor.

Although Don did not use the term globalization, many of the things that he talked about, and the feelings they evoked, reflect anxieties about the transformation of Australia from a country with a perceived national economy and guiding social democratic state, to one that was more open to the world, and based around notions of intense competitiveness and greater individualism. Widespread competitiveness, rather than mutuality and pulling together for the same cause, was perceived by Don as the source of Australia's decline. People had stopped thinking like a nation, and were now thinking simply as individuals.

Contrast Don's experience with Dora's, a Chinese Australian born in the late 1960s, who was 20 years old when she was first interviewed in the late 1980s. Although born and educated in Australia, she, like many Australians of the post-War period, had experienced the displacement of migration. Her parents, both Chinese but born in two different countries, arrived as adults in Australia, and she had lived in three of Australia's major cities. She had spent time in Singapore where her mother, now separated from her father, lived with her wealthy extended family.

Dora's experience of identity was far less straightforward and settled than Don's, and it was far less clearly national. Although close to her father, she felt that his "Chineseness," in particular his traditional views about family and gender roles, and his industriousness, created a distance between them. Growing up and educated in Australia, she felt that she could not connect with his formative experience. Her father wanted a traditional Chinese family where parents were an ongoing part of the child's life, including the life of friendship, work, and marriage. She wanted to escape, to be herself, to be free of such constraining bonds.

While Dora did not feel or identify as Chinese, she did not feel or identify as Australian either. She preferred to see herself as a "person of the world." She claimed that she did not feel patriotic, and in fact viewed any patriotism with suspicion, feeling that it only segregated the people of the world from each other. (While Don could be quite critical of certain features of Australian nationalism, especially a propensity to chauvinism with a racist taint, unlike Dora he was not suspicious of national identity as such.)

The Australia that Dora described was a far more fragmented place than it had been for Don. Part of this was a result of greater cultural and ethnic diversity, with different subcultures — ethnic, youth, even unemployed and peripherally employed countercultures — leading relatively separate lives, with little connection with each other. This was certainly Dora's own experience, as one of the long-term unemployed living a life far removed from the lives of those engaged in the working world, and from what she knew as the lack of interaction between Australia's different ethnic groups, separate from each other and from what was, for Dora, a vaguely perceived cultural mainstream. It was also more difficult to comprehend or to even think about a greater whole that encapsulated these separate and competing interests.

Australia was not really alive for Dora: it was a kind of empty signifier, a vision of vast space where individuals were free to get on with their lives. "People in Australia seem to go off and do their own thing…, there seems to be space for being individual here." This emphasis on the individual was crucial to Dora's life narrative, in a way that it never was for Don. Dora looked upon society as an amalgam of individuals, sometimes involved in loosely defined subcultures, going about their lives, pursuing their own aims and desires. She was far less connected than someone like Don with any sense of a public world beyond herself. This absence of a broader concept of society or nation, or even social structure, meant that she took almost no interest in the political issues of the day, and when questioned, simply did not have the knowledge to express an opinion. While Australia was for Dora a place where life was easier than it was in other places that she had visited — the state provision of welfare made life better in Australia, and Dora had immediate experience of this having recently emerged from a long period on the dole — this did not, however, give her a sense of national pride.

Dora's feelings of dislocation, of not really connecting with anything lasting, were, at least in part, a result of migration and familial breakdown. When I reinterviewed Dora recently, she explained that her family, in part because of her mother's mental breakdown, her father's "Confucian" silence, and her parents' separation, had not really equipped her and her brother for independent life outside the family home: thus, the more idiosyncratic and personal features of Dora's predicament. But like all personal stories, Dora's is at the same time a social story. It is one version of the experience of globalization: about people, and nuclear families, on the move and what can happen to them when they enter different cultural contexts away from broader familial and social networks. These are tendencies experienced by many people in societies that demand they be flexible and not too tied to any job or location.

What became apparent when interviewing the older Dora, however, was that although much in her life had not changed — she was still, in a sense free floating, living her life outside institutions — the nation framed her experience and her feelings about political and social issues, such as they were, far more than did any notion of her place among global humanity. Although she had worked sporadically as a computer programmer and had been involved with Internet companies — she was one of Reich's and Hannerz's "symbolic-analysts" — her world was far more local than one might have expected. When she communicated with people through the Internet, they were people in Australia, and even more specifically people living in and around her own city. She had never spent much time in other countries and apparently felt no great desire to do so. She had a curiosity about the specific ways that Australians debated things like immigration, refugees, multiculturalism, and indigenous issues. While she did not refer explicitly to a sense of Australianness, nearly all of her reference points centered on Australia, and it was clear that for all intents and purposes Australia was her most important moral community.

The life and experiences of Nina, a young woman of Sri Lankan background studying to be a nurse when interviewed at the beginning of the 1990s, parallel those of Dora in significant ways, although they diverge in other particulars. Nina was born in Sri Lanka but migrated with her parents at a young age, first to Singapore, and was now settled in Australia. Nina was about the same age as Dora, and like Dora, she lived between two cultural identities. Sri Lanka, its cultural traditions and, especially important for Nina, its close-knit family structure, formed a vantage point from which she viewed Australia: more so, given her childhood experiences there, than Singapore had for Dora.

The comparison between Sri Lanka and Australia was both positive and negative. While she seemed to miss the physical and emotional closeness of family in Sri Lanka — experienced in later years on return visits — she was otherwise bored with the pace of life and the passivity she perceived there. In Australia, things happened much more quickly, and she reveled in that faster pace of life. On the other hand, in Australia, she felt more isolated, and she never felt the sense of intense belonging she had sometimes experienced in Sri Lanka: "The thing is when I went there [Sri Lanka] you just get this incredible sense of, I can't explain it, it's just belonging or something, you know, it's a sense of family, you just can't get it here."

The break with her parents was cultural and generational, and was felt passionately. She had to keep much of her life from them: "I really live just an incredibly double life…," she said. Partly, this was about being a young daughter, any young daughter, but her peculiar circumstances also impinged. She had to lead such a double life because it was not the life expected of a good Sri Lankan girl, in her parents' estimation of that kind of person. Thus, she had to partake of a sophisticated performance involving subterfuge, hiding aspects of herself and activities, and climbing out of windows in order to frequent the nightclubs that she loved.

Collective identity — ethnic, national — was, for Nina, enigmatic, even felt as a burden. Here were her rather halting and confused feelings when asked to describe her national or racial identity:

Oh, that's hard too, because I'm not, I'm Sri Lankan as in blood Sri Lankan but not the cultural, no way, it's far too backward for me, far too dark ages. I have nothing to do with it, not religion or anything, but then again I don't have, I don't have, oh I don't think, oh this is hard because, I don't know, my identity I think is very much, it's not anything to do with my background… Oh,

maybe my surroundings are here but then, you know like I
don't think it has anything to do with people around. I can't, I
don't know. It's definitely not Sri Lankan, not much anyway, not
that I can identify. But Australian? I still don't think Australian is
me either, you know. Is there an in between? Is there somewhere else like England or something? Oh God I don't know. I
don't think I have a national identity to tell you the truth. I don't
think I'm Australian and I don't think I'm Sri Lankan as in the
sense that, you know, culturally or anything else, religiously...

But Nina did not experience this lack of a collective identity as
something negative. At worst, she felt ambivalent. As she per-
ceptively pointed out, "if you don't have it [national identity],
if you've never had it, you don't know the difference anyway
so its not that important, to me anyway. It's not important to
me to have a national identity... I don't know, it's too trivial,
too small, it's a very, very small, minor thing." Perhaps, it
would be nice to have a more defined national identity, she
mused, but she definitely did not want a Sri Lankan identity,
and nor did she want an Australian one. She did not want to
belong to Australian culture, she said, "because there really
isn't that much of a specific culture in Australia, because it's so
multicultural."

In Nina's eyes, Australia was fragmented into different, and
mostly separate, cultures from many different places, and she
did not perceive any dominant cultural core within that mix.
The point is not whether there is such a core culture, but that
from her vantage point she did not perceive one. "What's so
unique about Australia," she said, "there's no other place the
same really, so many different cultures." Having a "certificate
saying they're Australians" meant very little. It certainly did not

mean that Australia could be defined by any one sense of cultural belonging, or by a common culture. Greeks, Vietnamese, Turks, Sri Lankans: they each lived in their own cultural enclaves. Perhaps, she commented, there could eventually be one culture in Australia, "maybe in thousands of years," although she could not see how it could happen. On the other hand, multiculturalism, in the sense of different cultures maintaining their differences in Australia and leading separate lives, disturbed her. She would have liked to see more mixing between the different ethnic groups.

How then did Nina view and experience her own self within such a context? She, like Dora, saw herself primarily as an individual; but unlike Dora, she currently felt thwarted, by her present restrictive circumstances, in the pursuit of her individuality. Her parents, her nursing course and the other students, the institutions where she worked part-time, other people generally, all frustrated her pursuit of what she wanted. She admitted to feeling an incredible rage welling up inside, against others, and against her own current circumstances.

Nina is, in certain respects, an example of the consumer self (Bauman 1998: chap. 4), drifting through nightclubs, obsessed with clothes, overspending, and then having to find ways to manage her debts. She spoke at great length about the nightclubs she went to, the clothes she bought, the way that she loved, above most things, to lose herself dancing all night. At the same time, she gave vent to her rage in the anonymity of those same nightclubs by lashing out at those she felt had directly or indirectly offended her.

Nina made it clear that these things (clothes, nightclubs) were a central part of her life. The clothes marked her out as an individual, and she was extremely competitive when measuring herself against others: "I just like dressing up, it makes me feel good, you know. I don't know why, it's just probably … I just like being a little above everybody else… I love to stand out, I usually do." The nightclubs allowed her to shine. For the same reason, she abhorred the way that she lost her sense of individuality when she donned a nursing uniform.

As for personal ambition, her most passionate aim was to become rich. She was fascinated by the mysterious upper class that she viewed, from a distance as she drove in her car, in wealthy Melbourne suburbs like Toorak. She wanted to be rich like them, but she did not know what steps she would have to take to get there. The nursing profession meant nothing to her. It was simply a stepping stone, something her father chose for her when she still listened to him, for want of knowing what else to do. Her life would not be defined, it would seem, by such professional involvements and in serving the public. Nina had no connection with or interest in the political world. As she put it, "politics have never really interested me that much." Political issues were "out there," not her responsibility and largely not her concern.

Comparing the experiences of Dora and Nina on the one hand with those of Don on the other, one notices a number of significant differences. First, Dora and Nina perceive and pursue a radical rupture between the generations. There is no smooth transition from one generation to the other — a kind of passing of the baton the way Don experienced it — but rather a severance, a striking out on one's own, as if one had the responsibility to remake oneself, and that the older generation's experience and knowledge were irrelevant, and even felt as an obstruction. For both Nina and Dora, immigration provoked this generational discontinuity, as it gave rise to new cultural expectations and experiences that served to sever them from the more traditional past of their parents' world. But their life experiences are also indicative of the changing moral frameworks of the late modern globalizing world, and of the expansion of possibilities and personal freedom, including the freedom to be an individual.

Second, we see a decoupling of self from ethnic or national community — no doubt in each of their cases exacerbated, again, by the experience of migration and subsequent identity confusion. But in its place, we do not find a point of broad connection with the public world. Australian society, at least as Dora and Nina saw it, was an atomized place where free-floating individuals must use their own personal repertoire of skills to find their own way. Third, for both Dora and Nina it is as if society has no center, but rather is characterized by fragmentation — in both their cases, the society lacks coherence, mainly because of its multiculturalism.

Finally, compared with Don they each felt less responsible for the rest of society. They were each *moving through society*, rather than seeing themselves meshed with it. They were trying to survive and get on as individuals, and this seemed to exhaust their energies. The public world, or a sense of the broader collective, whether national or anything else, had less grip on them. Dora summed this attitude up when she stressed that individuals had a duty to themselves to strive to be happy, and to think of their inner needs before they began thinking about contributing to society: "Like what a policewoman said to me once, 'Why don't you contribute to society?'... . Those sorts of attitudes I don't really have. I sort of more think every person...sort of every person for their own, it's more important for every person to be happy I think, within themselves and do what they think, you know, is reasonable."

Dora and Nina might be considered postnational selves. The nation, as such, meant little to them. They had no viable framework through which to imagine it. Their experiences tell us something about the new conditions in which nationality is lived by some people in Australia. But these are not the only characteristic experiences of national identity, or lack of it, in contemporary Australian society.

Wayne, a nonimmigrant Australian of Dora's and Nina's generation, was a young mechanic in the process of setting up his own business when he was first interviewed in the late 1980s. He had grown up in the northern suburbs of his city in a predominantly Anglo-Celtic social milieu, middle-class enough to be sent to a small private school, but by no means wealthy. He still lived at home and closely identified with his parents, especially with his father. There was a long family tradition of involvement in the car business, which Wayne saw himself as continuing. Apart from the genuine passion he felt about cars, it gave Wayne a strong sense of his place in Australian society.

Wayne represented a vivid example of a robust sense of Australianness being reproduced in a city suburb as it might have been a generation earlier. He was secure in his social milieu and felt no great desire to step outside of it. In Wayne's case, generational rootedness in Australia gave rise to an assured sense of nationality and belonging. Like Mick, he had a clear sense of an old Australian type, living for the most part out in the national heartland of the bush, which he visited frequently on family excursions, but who also found expression among those who fought for Australia, and among many ordinary people like himself. He liked to talk to older men in pubs about their war experiences, and through them he felt a connection with Australia's history. Well-versed in Australian folklore and myths surrounding the nation, Wayne's powerful sense of Australian national identity was built on a generational identification, especially with those who had served in war, including some of his ancestors. He was annoyed if anyone disparaged that identity, through demonstrating, for example, during days of national celebration, or during war commemoration marches.

When interviewed again in 2003, his circumstances had changed — he now ran a thriving business, and was married with children — but he maintained the same sense of self-assured Australianness. Although he worked in an industry that had become far more transnational after the 1980s, with automotive parts and accessories being manufactured in different parts of the world where labor was far cheaper, and then imported into Australia, this somehow had little impact on the way that he thought of himself or about Australia. There was a sense, however, that he was worried about the impact of new developments, expressed as a contrast between the old Australia of his suburb, and his past, and the new multicultural Australia he stepped into when he went to the suburb where his business was located:

> Well I think there's problems with, I'm not actually a racist person, but when you work in Brunswick and you live in the Rosanna, Heidelberg sort of area, there's two completely different sorts of things going on in the streets. At home it just seems the same as when I was growing up, except I'm the one doing what my parents were doing. You're trying to renovate a house and you're trying to find time to play and all the rest of it,

and nothing really seems to be that much different over that way. When you come to this side of my world, anyway, it just tends to be that there's these ethnic groups that just bond together and they're sort of almost too powerful in their own little thing. They're just like gangs. I reckon that's a major problem. *[The Italians and Greeks?]* They're not the problems. *[That's something you were talking about.]* Oh no no, the Lebanese and the Muslims and all that in this area particularly are taking over. I don't think the Asian population's too much of a problem in Australia. There's always bad guys in that sort of stuff. It's the Lebanese. Well not so much them but the Muslim, whatever that encompasses.

I will return to this issue in the next chapter when I discuss the new complexity of social space and the way that individuals live their nationalities in relation to that complexity.

Even among first- and second-generation immigrant Australians there are experiences of identity, including Australian national identity, far different from those of Dora and Nina. The same globalizing forces, including immigration, that for Dora and Nina produced experiences of the breakdown of generational familial relationships, societal fragmentation, and national disorientation can result in a person putting together a much more coherent identity, mixing a sense of Australianness with a sense of cosmopolitanism.

Katerina, a young Greek-Australian teacher working in a private boys' grammar school, was who older Australians might have once called a new Australian, or an ethnic Australian. She was part of the Greek diaspora that formed such an important first wave in Australia's ethnic diversification. Her mother came to Australia as a young girl with her parents in the 1940s and had, in Katerina's words, "become acculturated." Katerina's father left Greece on his own at a time of uncertainty, in the 1950s, when he was in his mid-twenties and wanted to get on in the world, away from Greece with its repression of dissent and its lack of business opportunities.

Katerina's experience of her own identity is not unlike that of many others in the period of "people on the move," where identities are not simply bound by the nation. But unlike Dora or Nina, Katerina strongly identified as an Australian. She felt no conflict between this identification and her identification as a Greek: "A large part of me is Greek. I'll occasionally prattle off in Greek without even knowing it. I might say something, I might do something, I might be Greek occasionally. Now that is a part of me, I am proud of that." Although her most powerful sense of home was in Australia, in her suburb, and her city, she also felt connected to Greece, especially to the places where her family history was sedimented. Unlike other Greeks she knew, torn between two cultures in Australia, she felt that she had found the right balance between maintaining a sense of Greekness and being Australian. She understood the difficulties involved in cultural adjustment. She had seen those of her fellows who, brought up in more traditionalist families than her own, had sought to maintain a strong sense of Greekness within Australian society, but had only succeeded in becoming stranded.

Katerina never really had doubts about her Australianness, and this was confirmed when she first visited Greece as a teenager: "I suppose I just always thought I was [Australian] but it was just reinforced when I went overseas and was told that I was Australian or I could be easily picked out. It was something that I think was innate, it was always there, there wasn't a question as to whether I was or I wasn't." When asked what came to mind when she thought of Australia, her response was immediate and emphatic: "A nation, a country, my home."

Her class position and the particular character of her family's immigrant experience were influential in the construction of that identity. Katerina was privileged, from a well-off middle class family. Her father moved up the class scale in Australia, becoming a successful retailer. Katerina grew up in a middle-class suburb that was definitely not an "ethnic suburb" like the nearby inner city working class suburbs. This was, in a sense, a form of family assimilation: they were not surrounded by other Greeks. This did not mean that Katerina did not grow up in a Greek-Australian community: her father was active in Greek education, she went to Greek school at nights and on weekends, and her social group had remained predominantly Greek. However, her family's experience contributed to the ease with which she moved between Greek and the wider Australian society. Unlike Dora's and Nina's families, Katerina's family provided strong nurturing and warmth: she still discussed openly any major decisions affecting her life with her parents and her brother.

Katerina's sense of Australianness was deep, and multilayered. It allowed for the coexistence of what might be considered by some as mutually exclusive identities. She felt a powerful connection with the Australian landscape: in addition to being a history teacher, she taught geography and was intensely aware of Australia's distinctive and delicate geographical formation. She also felt connected to traditional national myths, like those underpinning the Anzac Day ceremonies at her school, which she found very moving. Her identification with the school as an institution meant that she identified with the loss of the school's former pupils through war, and through them, with the losses of their families and the Australian community. She had felt patriotic during some of the celebrations for Australia's Bicentenary.

Katerina embraced the story that Australians, and in particular some of Australia's leaders, attempted to tell themselves about their identity from about the 1970s, after white Australia had pretty much run its course: that Australian identity was multicultural. Multicultural identity presents itself as a form of identity ideally suited to a globalizing world, a theme that I take up in the next chapter. For the remainder of this chapter, I want to reflect more theoretically on some of the expressions and experiences of Australian national identity apparent among the people discussed above.

At one point during the 1990s, after ten or so years of dramatic social, cultural, and economic change, it seemed that everyone in Australia was talking about the "problem" of Australian identity: it was weak, spiritually bankrupt, in need of renovation, reinvention or defense, in crisis, and under threat from one thing or another. At least this is the impression one might have gained from opening the newspapers, watching television or listening to the radio. Out in the suburban and country homes it might have been a different story. For many people, it is enough to worry about personal or household finances, raising families or keeping them together, let alone be bothered with debates and disputes about national identity. Scratch a little below the surface with a lot of those people who do not write or contribute to the cultural debates in the various media, however, and you find that there is a concern with national identity, even if it has to jostle with other issues and concerns that might be more immediately apparent. Sometimes, it is simply the assumed background against which people conduct their daily lives, becoming overt only when stirred by someone or something. During the 1990s the questioning of Australia's national identity was stimulated by debates about immigration, multiculturalism, republicanism, and settler/Aboriginal relations. It was also stimulated by the changes and social disruption caused by the reorientation of the state, the opening up of Australia to the global economy, and the new emphasis upon competition.

National identity, in Australia and elsewhere, remains a powerful, perhaps the most powerful, form of collective identity. It is not the only such form by any stretch but, for the very reasons that writers like Anthony Smith (1987, 1995) and Benedict Anderson (1983) have cited — especially the ways that it took over from earlier imaginings of community, destiny, fate and communal and personal immortality, and organized and responded to collective memory — national identity became from about the nineteenth century onward the most important way of imagining sovereignty and community. Nothing has yet replaced it, even if writers as distinguished as Eric Hobsbawm (1990: 182–183) have claimed that with intensifying globalization, the era of the nation is passing into history, and that national belonging will give way to other forms of identity somewhere in the future.

There is plenty of evidence to suggest that Australians continue to feel and value a strong sense of national identity. National surveys in Australia indicate that large majorities feel "very proud" to be Australian, and cross-national studies have shown that Australians report levels of national pride, which rank among the highest in the world. Surveys also indicate that large majorities of Australians feel that it is very important to be patriotic, and feel that Australians should be more patriotic (for summaries of these studies, see Phillips 1998). Such studies are suggestive of the ongoing salience of national identity for Australians; but are there ways that contemporary globalization impacts upon Australians' experience of national identity? Has Australian national identity been reshaped or affected by globalization? The answer to these questions will depend, among other things, upon where one is situated within Australian social space, and in relation to the impact of globalizing trends.

Australian national identity has always been a complex affair, with republican and imperial strands competing from the nineteenth century onward. For some, Australian national identity was almost inseparable from British national identity. For others, Australian identity had to be forged in relationship with Australian land, and needed to be distinguished from British national identity. To further complicate matters, Australia's colonial history remains as a kind of underlying support for regional identities competing with a vision of a more centralized, Canberra-, Melbourne-, or Sydney- dominated identity and set of concerns. Before there was an Australian national identity there were important colonial identities, and these sometimes resurface as state rivalries over the nation's resources, or over the center's (i.e., Canberra's) right to dictate terms to the periphery (i.e., Queensland, Western Australia, or the far north). They can also compete with a sense of wider national identity, with people feeling, especially in certain contexts, that they are Queenslanders, Victorians, Tasmanians, Western Australians, South Australians, New South Welshmen, and even Northern Territorians, before they are Australians. At the substate level, and crisscrossing the nation, there is the well-known city/country divide, with those in the country, in particular, farmers and graziers, viewing themselves as the true heart of the nation, and feeling aggrieved at perceived or actual economic and status losses.

Today, there is competition between those who feel strongly that Australia's Anglo-Celtic heritage needs to be defended against those advocating a more multicultural Australian identity, and those who feel that Australian identity must embrace its multicultural nature and forge deeper links between the indigenous and nonindigenous populations. There are others who feel that Australian identity is a side issue, and that what really matters is that Australians become democratic citizens of the world, with a global or cosmopolitan identity (Castles et al. 1988). National identity, whether in Australia or elsewhere, is viewed by such denizens of cosmopolitan global identity as nostalgic and outdated, even retarding and dangerous, in the face of globalizing trends.

The nation, therefore, means different things to different people, and different conceptions and lived experiences of national identity coexist under the same national umbrella. Although this has always been so, intensified globalization has served to diversify these characteristic orientations, providing, for some people, new avenues for the expression of Australian national identity and an actual loosening of the hold of national identity for others.

Some theorists write of the emergence of postnational or cosmopolitan selves associated with the complex forms of existence in the period of intensified globalization. Theorists like Anthony Giddens (1991, 1994), Ulrich Beck (1992, 1997), and Zygmunt Bauman (1997, 2001) have explored and analyzed this phenomenon under the concept of individualization. They argue that we live in the era of the do-it-yourself personal biography, where the self is less constrained by traditional categories of gender, class, ethnicity, and nation. Identities, they argue, have become more fragmentary, more compulsive, and impulsive. In keeping with the hyperreflexivity of contemporary globalizing societies, individuals must keep themselves constantly open to change, including ongoing personal transformation.

The closely related phenomenon of "cosmopolitanization," Beck argues, is a consequence of these new conditions. The breakup of old contexts and the intensification of global flows result in the horizon of individuals reaching out beyond traditional community. Individuals inevitably become more cosmopolitan as their identities become more flexible. According to Beck, this is related to the effective disappearance, in any meaningful sense, of national identities. "The cosmopolitan project," Beck (2000: 90) argues, "contradicts and replaces the nation-state project" (see also Boyne 2001).

It is worth delineating what might be more than one set of processes here. The cosmopolitan self implies a level of cultural mastery: the capacity to lose oneself in an alien culture or cultures depends upon the capacity to experience one's own culture from a certain distance, which implies that one has a masterful grasp of it (Hannerz 1996: chap. 9). To what extent such cosmopolitanism depends upon a fundamental security in one's own national identity is an open question (Améry 1986).[1] A postnational self might be very different to that, more a case of disorientation and fragmentation that implies no such mastery of any culture. Flexibility, the constant reinvention of one's personal biography, can lead to chronic insecurity, a loss of a sense of depth to life, and, as Richard Sennett (1998) has recently argued in *The Corrosion of Character*, to the loss of moral bearings.

Moreover, these processes are best seen as pressures and tendencies, not as completed social transformations of the experience of the self. If there are important new tendencies — of accelerated change, flexibility, fragmentation, and disembedding — affecting the experience of the self, then we have to consider other processes with which they intersect, like tradition (or reinvented tradition), resistance, and the pull of committment to place. Furthermore, we must take into account the uneven spread of such tendencies within and between globalizing societies. There will be individuals and groups of people, for example, where these tendencies are more and less pronounced. This will also be the case for countries taken as a whole.

In this chapter, I sought to illustrate some of these transformations by considering and comparing different ways of relating to the Australian nation in this period of intensified globalization. This was not exhaustive, rather more the beginning of an exploration of national identity under the impact of globalization that will be carried through in the remaining chapters of this book. It was necessarily impressionistic. There have been few qualitative studies of everyday experiences of Australian national identity (Phillips 1998: 283; Phillips and Smith 2000). The portraits were of individuals, although they are suggestive of broad patterns of experience.

Three

Carol was in her early forties when first interviewed in the late 1980s. Having left high school before completing the final year, she had married young. With her husband she helped manage a growing family business which, together with bringing up her children, consumed most of her time. Carol grew up in a regional town that had attracted a non-British immigrant population since the Second World War. She had lived there since the age of ten, for the most part happily and contentedly.

Carol was less articulate than some of our interviewees when it came to talking about multiculturalism. She preferred to speak of what she knew best — that is, through local knowledge. Though she had Italian ancestry on her mother's side, few would consider Carol an "ethnic Australian." Carol herself felt little connection to that Italian heritage. At school, though sometimes toying with the exoticism of being Italian, she fitted seamlessly into the Anglo-Celtic world, and was not identified by her school mates with the darker Europeans — the Greeks, Italians, and Yugoslavs — who started turning up at her school and in her town in the 1950s, and who were sometimes taunted by the other children.

Carol expressed little fear of "otherness." Though confined to her local surrounds, she roamed the world through the pages of *National Geographic* and was fascinated by the different ways that other people lived. She and her husband would employ anyone in their business, no matter what the ethnic background, as long as they were good workers. She abhorred prejudice: "Oh I get cross with other people saying things about certain races. Often they're quite ignorant remarks anyway, prejudiced, and I don't like that. I don't like seeing anybody not get a fair go, I get quite cross about it."

When she turned to the issue of multiculturalism, her impulse was to move away from the abstract and to focus on the individual case. For Carol, multiculturalism was essentially a question of people fitting other people in, given time and opportunity. It involved giving people the chance to adapt, and giving Australian society time to make the slow adaptations. She saw many advantages of the influx of different cultures into Australia. "I mean, goodness me, haven't we come a long way since all of the migrants arrived," she enthused. While she seemed to have in mind quasibiological notions about improving the stock and avoiding interbreeding in a small population, what she mainly meant by this was the way that the influx had brought in something new to the culture.

Carol did not like to think about the possible disadvantages of multiethnic immigration, at least not in the abstract. She went on what she herself had seen and experienced, the way that things had worked out in the end. Certainly, she said, the Greeks were "really looked on rather badly" and the Italians were at first considered "dark and different and rather aggressive," but these days they were "accepted quite readily." She spoke fondly of the Laotians and Vietnamese she had met and liked. She would have no truck with the negative stereotypes other people sometimes used: "It's just people's attitudes to them that stirs up trouble." When asked about concerns expressed in the media and by some politicians during the

1980s, about Vietnamese refugees and the general level of Asian intake in the immigration program, her response was measured. Her concern was with what she perceived as the concentration of Asians in the city: "We were in Sydney recently and in one section we felt it was just about 'Spot the Aussie,' it was so many of these Asians, whether they just happened to be all in this one group in the area where we were, I'm not sure, but it did look a bit overpowering." On the other hand, she understood how and why it happens:

> But, I mean, why can't they be given a chance too? I mean, where are they going to go? And, quite often, you know, all the ones I know here are delightful people, really quite gentle. Perhaps if they were spread out more throughout Australia rather than simply lumped all together in cities, but I know they like to stick together in their own little groups. And there's been lots of talk about how aggressive they are and that, but I really don't think per ratio of population that they're any worse than a lot of Australians or other migrants that are here. It just seems to be blown up a bit, to me.

Since the 1980s when, as I explain below, multiculturalism became controversial, the voices from "old" Anglo-Celtic Australia have ranged from anger and distrust of multiculturalism, to grudging and enthusiastic support. Some like Arthur, a late middle-aged Anglo-Celtic Australian insurance company executive interviewed at the end of the 1980s, expressed doubts about multiculturalism:

> Well, you see, I am a little hostile on the one hand to people who come from overseas and want to immediately change

Australia. I don't mean by that that there won't be some changes in, you know, eating habits and all these things. But multiculturalism ... is something that needs to be very well clarified. I think it would be an enormous mistake for Australia to have multiculturalism as something which meant that you had Greek communities and Italian communities and Japanese communities all living in those sort of, well, we won't say ghettoes because they probably have plenty of money, but in their own little community ways where they have their own languages and their own customs and all that. I don't think that would be a good thing for Australia at all. And that doesn't mean to say we can't benefit — and we already have benefited — from the skills and diversities and so forth of all these people that come in, but I want them to come in and become Australians in the more or less conventional role that we think of as Australians: they speak English, they go to English-speaking schools, they conform with our laws, they become our citizens, they acknowledge what we acknowledge, they drive on the left and, you know, *I mean they do the same bloody things that we do.*

Arthur's comments reflect the ongoing strength of the assimilationist trend in Australian political culture. They also reflect a fairly widespread attitude to the presence of visible ethnic groupings in Australian society: to view them warily, sometimes fearfully, and to consider them a potential threat to cohesion of the nation (Jupp 1992: 141). Despite a proven lack of the development of "ethnic enclaves," let alone "ghettoes" in Australian society (Jupp et al. 1990), the fear that these are developing, or have already developed, because of immigration and multiculturalism, is a common Australian complaint. As

Kel, the shearer discussed at the beginning of the previous chapter, put it when I spoke to him in 2003: "As far as multi-culturalism's concerned, it worries me where whole suburbs in cities can become ... like a new Vietnam or a new Cambodia or a new Thailand or whatever. That worries me because that's only going to breed racism. They should be mixing."

On the other hand, it is apparent even in the critical comments of Arthur that he is not really against multiculturalism as such: as he says, it needs to be carefully defined and handled. Others like Don (discussed in Chapter Two) were basically supportive of what they considered the inevitable shift to a more multicultural Australia. Don was intensely annoyed by what he called the "ill-informed grandstanding" of prominent Australian historians like Geoffrey Blainey and others who, during the 1980s, criticized the level of Asian immigration (see my later discussion of such critique). Although Don lamented the disappearance of an older, more "homely," Australia — having grown up happily and securely within its embrace — he felt that Australia would now benefit from a wider understanding and appreciation of the cultures that surround it in the region, and which now formed a significant proportion of the national population. Don recognized the finer attributes of the Australia in which he grew up, such as its commitments to egalitarianism and social justice, and the cohesiveness and solidarity of its striving, and intensely local, communities. But the world and Australia had not stood still, and Australians had to recognize the changed circumstances in which they now found themselves. The problem, according to Don, was that Anglo-Celtic Australia was not multicultural in spirit, too closed in on itself and prone to conceitedness and a false sense of racial superiority. If Australia was to survive, and moreover to avoid becoming the "white trash of the Pacific," it had to become more multicultural in attitude, and less insular. It needed to think more clearly about its region and how it was enmeshed there. Australians as a group, he felt, needed a "good injection of other people's virtues."

In a parallel way, Alan, a Christian socialist in his fifties with wide experience in Australia and abroad, saw within his own lifetime a great improvement to Australian society stemming from its increased multiculturalism. As he put it in the late 1980s, "I just think that multiculturalism or whatever it is, the coexistence and mutual enrichment of a lot of different races and cultures in Australia, is highly desirable and everyone's enriched by it." Alan had a robust commitment to Australia and at the same time an outward-looking view of the world and interconnectedness, showing how nationalism and internationalism are not necessarily contradictory. Looking at the debates about immigration and multiculturalism of the 1980s, he pointed out that the critics of multiculturalism, with their dire warnings of strife through cohabitation of ethnic identities in national territory, had sanitized Australia's own past. "Especially important in this regard," Alan commented, "is that Geoffrey Blainey has set criteria as to the desirable nature of immigrants and that it is that one should be prepared either to marry them, or to pray with them, and that this is necessary to give that homogeneity to the nation which would enable it to fight a war with an aggressor." By these very criteria, he pointed out, Australia was fundamentally divided in the first half of the twentieth century, up until the early 1950s. In his view Catholics and Protestants in Australia were as culturally divided as Anglo-Celtic was claimed to be from non-Anglo-Celtic society today. He remembered that in his own childhood he and his schoolmates delightedly screamed out at the Catholic school-children across the road: "States, states ring the bells, Catholics, Catholics go to hell!" Prior to doing National Service and going to university, he had had virtually no contact with Catholics. As a young man he would never have dreamed of marrying a Catholic and recalled that his mother's father "had told her that he preferred to see her in her grave rather than marry a Catholic, *even though his own mother was an Irish Catholic.*" Despite that, people from different ethnic and religious backgrounds managed to come together to defend Australia at a time of crisis, during the Second World War.

Alan viewed the change to a more multicultural society in Australia as very positive. At the other extreme, there had been, in his view, too much recent idealization of Britain and all things British. He had worked with and lived among people from a variety of backgrounds and felt that, based on this experience, he had nothing to fear from "multiracial humanity." As he put it "I have no fears or worries or anxieties about my granddaughters marrying a Kenyan or a Thai or a Nepalese or anything else."

Other "old" Australians felt more certain of the virtues of Anglo-Celtic Australia, and viewed multiculturalism as a more subtle and, in some ways superficial, influence. In his early thirties and working for an employers' association in a rural area when first interviewed in 1989, Andrew sat confidently at what he felt was the center of Australian national life. His family, with Irish and British Protestant roots, had been in Australia for five or six generations. He described himself as "a long-standing Australian":

In that sense I don't feel any cultural attachment or political attachment or anything to any other country. So if I'm not Australian I'm stateless. I don't feel any dual nationality at all.

He was educated in one of Melbourne's elite private schools and belonged to "the moral middle class" as writers like Judith Brett (1992, 2003) and Janet McCalman (1993) call it. Members of this social grouping, McCalman writes, "placed themselves as the center — they were the backbone of the nation; those 'with a stake in the country'; the shoulders upon which responsibility for the well-being of society actually fell" (1993: 136).

Australian identity was an easy fit that Andrew wore lightly. Indeed, he played down the very idea and importance of national identity. "In my opinion," he said, "all that countries and governments are is something that's necessary so that individuals can live together in the world ... I don't think there's anything sacrosanct or wonderful about the idea of nationhood." One of Australia's virtues, according to Andrew, was that it lacked a "great national ethos." A related virtue was that "it's not a strong ideological society." He saw these attributes as sources of Australia's real strength, and in particular of its capacity to "absorb" wave upon wave of immigrants: "maybe that's why we've been able to absorb so many cultures, because I don't think, really deep down, that we're very chauvinistic about Australian society."

In Andrew's portrayal, changes throughout Australia's history had been gradual and incremental rather than dramatic, and these included the changes resulting from the post-Second World War program of immigration. Andrew was in no sense embattled. He did not feel that sense of change and loss that other Anglo-Celtic Australians have lamented (Dixson 1999). One of the more interesting things about Australian society, according to Andrew, was the way that each influx of immigrants has adapted to the "Protestant" Australian traditions:

> It's an amazing thing, actually, that strikes me in this country: ethnic groups, hundreds of different ethnic groups, and really, a good proportion of the population is born outside the country, and yet the moral norms seem to be pretty constant, you know, we haven't become Muslim fundamentalist, or anything else. I mean, you might say that the moral norms aren't all that terrific but it's amazing how that influx over thirty years, how really it still remains, you know, a Protestant moral society in a sense.

While Andrew recognized that, at least on the surface, Australia had a much more multicultural feel to it than, say, the Japan he knew from his business trips, Australian multiculturalism was, he felt, very much at the level of appearances. In his view Australia was so good because it was basically an assimilatory culture. "I think it's unrealistic to say people forget their cultures in the first generation or second generation even," he said, but on the other hand he believed that "the history of immigration to this country, and anywhere else for that matter, is that, as generations go by, there are changes to the adherence to previous cultures."

Unlike Nina and Dora, who as I showed in the last chapter perceived Australia as a society without a center, based on ethnic diversity, Andrew perceived a vivid mainstream or core culture, upon which all else rested and proceeded in Australia. He was so identified with the "core culture," and he felt that it was so strong and enduring, that identity became for him almost a nonissue.

When Andrew was interviewed again recently, he was more openly supportive of the concept of multiculturalism:

> Personally I'm a great supporter of multiculturalism, in the sense of cultural diversity. Multiculturalism is a term that's sort of become politically bad. But in terms of cultural diversity I think it's a great strength. It's an enormous strength for this country. It's convenient for politicians to make it bad I suppose. But the term doesn't worry me either way. I tend to use the term cultural diversity because I think it's more descriptive than multiculturalism and I'm often using it in the context of business where cultural diversity in a business is highly advantageous. Sometimes it's essential. But I don't have any problem with the term multiculturalism. To me it's a term of tolerance and allowing people to follow whatever views, practices and beliefs, as long as it's consistent with the general harmony of the society. So I suppose I'm one of those ones that says as long as you don't bring your feuds and your violence then that's fine.

He also placed a greater emphasis on the way that waves of immigrants had made their impact upon the core culture: "I think over generations, obviously people who have come here, by the time they get to the second and third generation there's substantive change. But I think that they also imprinted their change on the society." One of the great and important improvements, he felt, was the injection of multilingualism into the society. We could use our linguistic and cultural complexity to deal better with the rest of the world and to forge business, social, and cultural links, in a more globally organized environment.

Henry, on the other hand, was more openly critical of the general drift of Australian society toward multicultural policy. Henry was a bank employee in his late twenties, a political conservative from an Anglo-Celtic background. When interviewed in the late 1980s, he perceived a very different sort of Australia taking shape to that of the past and did not like much of what he saw. On the face of it, he might seem a logical supporter of multiculturalism, and for the shift from white Australia to a more diverse Australia. He was middle-class, university educated, and had married a Chinese immigrant from Hong Kong. Instead, he was a disgruntled assimilationist nationalist.

Drawing on the experience of his wife's family, he felt that it was inevitable that some cultural traditions would be maintained by people who migrated to Australia. In fact, there was nothing wrong with that, as long as the immigrants committed themselves to Australia:

> Her whole family came out here in about 1966/67, sometime around about there. Now, they speak Chinese, they eat Chinese, they celebrate Chinese religion and festivals, but they're Australian, they were naturalized quite a long time ago, they have no intention ever of moving back to Hong Kong or China, their children all went to Australian schools and were encouraged to be Australian, and I think that's the right way to go.

Henry cited as one of the most important contemporary concerns in Australia the shift in public policy from assimilation to multiculturalism. He saw multicultural policy as economic madness: we simply could not afford to service the needs of the proliferating "subcultures" in Australia through culturally specific programs. He felt that governments were promoting the development of ethnic enclaves, and that there were real dangers in the development of conflicting loyalties within Australia's borders, which may result in disaster during any wars in the future. Multiculturalism, he believed, was driven by policy bureaucrats rather than by the people from the ethnic backgrounds whom it was meant to serve. Based on his own anecdotal evidence, and on his interaction with people from different ethnic backgrounds, he claimed to know that multiculturalism was not what those people wanted:

> And when I talk to friends of mine, for example, a guy I was having dinner with on Saturday night, he was from Lebanon and his parents took much the same approach. He doesn't like the idea of the so-called multicultural society where you have these Lebanese groups and Greeks and Chinese and Vietnamese, identifiable subcultures being promoted within Australia, and that is what is happening in the current political climate and I think that's a significant problem.

His perception of the problem with the move away from assimilation was that it had meant more people came to Australia without the intention of becoming Australians. "I'm very strongly against those people maintaining the primary bond to the society from which they've come rather than the society which they've joined," he explained.

When pushed to consider alternative viewpoints, and calling the multiculturalists' bluff (as he would see it), Henry demanded to know how Australian society had been in any way enriched by non-Anglo-Celtic cultures. They could not enrich mainstream society, he pointed out, if they remained as self-enclosed subcultures. He knew nothing about Yugoslav or Cambodian culture, so how had he been enriched by them, he asked? He resented ethnic "subcultures" for the way that they, supposedly, failed to open themselves up to the mainstream culture. And he was angry that the shift in government policy away from assimilation had, in his view, contributed to this "emerging" situation.

The other side of this resentment was Henry's willingness to embrace anyone, regardless of their ethnic background, and to learn something through his interaction with individuals, about other cultures, traditions and perspectives. (One can even sense in Henry's complaint — about ethnic cultures "closed" against him — a wish that he could benefit from knowing them better.) In other words, he displayed no apparent fear of "otherness" or diversity as such. Henry was a principled liberal assimilationist who would have nothing to do with the exclusion of anybody because of their color or culture, no matter what others thought of their capacity to fit into Australian society. He was deeply disappointed by Liberal Opposition leader John Howard's comments in 1988 about reducing the intake of Asian immigrants (see the quote and explanation below) and, as a member of the Liberal Party, he was disappointed at the party's general handling of its leader's comments, which, he argued, flew in the face of its policy and philosophy.

Even people from the groups sometimes singled out by Anglo-Celtic Australians as "too alien" to assimilate into Australian society, like Dora and Nina (both from Asian backgrounds), have stressed the problem of too much separatism in Australia's multicultural society, and have expressed the wish for more open and regular interaction between groups. "It seems a pity," Dora said, "that they [Asians, Italians, Greeks, etc.] seem to stick together more than mixing" though she accepted that ease of communication and the prejudices of Anglo-Celtic Australia contributed to that. Similarly, Nina felt that poor social mixing between groups was one of the negative features of Australia's multiculturalism: in her ideal society there would be more interaction between different communities.

Rosa, while openly supportive of multiculturalism, expressed this sense of unease about separatism. It is worth examining what stands behind it. Rosa was a second-generation Italian immigrant, in her early twenties when interviewed in the late 1980s. She had a deep experiential understanding of living in a multicultural society, developed through her experiences at school, in her ethnically diverse suburb, and through her community and church-based involvements. She saw multiculturalism as one of Australia's great attributes. One of the great things about Australia's ethnic diversity, she felt, was the way that it allowed Australians to experience the complexity of the world on their own doorstep. This was something she did not feel in Italy, which she found was far more monocultural when she had recently traveled there. (The same comment was made by the much older Frieda, an Italian immigrant who felt that living in the ethnic diversity of Australia meant "having the world at your fingertips.")

Rosa did not idealize any culture or ethnic group when considering capacity for racial tolerance. She knew from her own experience that Italians, and Europeans more generally in Australia, could be as racist and as unwelcoming as anybody else, including Anglo-Celtic Australians, especially when it came to dealing with the visibility of Asians on the street. Rosa actively sought a wide range of friends from different ethnic backgrounds. Living in the inner city of Melbourne, she had made friends with the sons and daughters of the Vietnamese boat people, and she was looking to people from other backgrounds with whom she could make friendly connections. At the time of the interviews, she was grappling with the difficulty of coming to terms with the Muslim and black African populations that were beginning to register as a presence on the streets of Melbourne. It concerned her that the lives of these people were almost a complete mystery to her. That was not as it should be in a multicultural society, she felt. She wanted to be able to identify, in some way, with the lives of these people.

This reaction is often misunderstood. Being able to identify means being able to understand and to interact with an Other at some level, to bring the Other into some meaningful relation with the self. This is an important way of calming social space, of making it less threatening or tension-filled. There is no doubt that one of the attractions of national belonging is in the way that it makes social and geographical space familiar and homely. It is not that Rosa needed to know everything about these "strange" people, or even that she needed to be engaged with them at an intensely social level. What was most important was that she came to understand something about them, so that her fear of the unknown was defused. This is also one of the most important Australian understandings of multiculturalism — a deep and harmonious engagement with diversity in public space.

It has been claimed by some critics (see, e.g., Betts 1988, 1999) that "multiculturalism" is mainly supported by cosmopolitan elites who have little to fear from the impact of diverse populations on their own daily lives, and that, should they feel materially or symbolically threatened by immigrants, they might not prove to be so tolerant. It is implied by such critique that the less privileged, or the working class, are less tolerant, and for good reason (for critique of this argument, see Jupp 2002: chap. 6). While not wanting to claim that there is no truth in such an argument, this should not lead one to underestimate the variety of feelings about and understanding of multiculturalism found among the less privileged in Australian society. Mark Peel (2003) has recently argued that people living in disadvantaged multiracial areas live multiculturalism deeply, and are well-versed in the practices of tolerance, perhaps more so than the middle classes who experience multiculturalism more vicariously.

Rob was from an old working class family. He was a tradesman employed in maintenance with the state railways, and a union representative. When interviewed in the late 1980s, he, his wife, and three children lived in a working class suburb where they had bought a house from his mother. Their economic situation was precarious and their lives had often been very difficult, the usual round of illness and death somehow magnified. Here, nevertheless, was Rob's rather upbeat description of living within the multicultural space of that suburb:

> You know, it's just a pretty good area. There's a certain amount of migrant population. We've got the people renting the house next door, they're Scottish. And we've got Italians, Australians, Germans — that's in our street. So, we've got a fair broad spread of 'em, cos you've got Asians, Greeks and you know

other Maltese and everything in the area. You know, there's a pretty broad spectrum.

He got on well with most of these people, but particularly with the Italians, who he felt shared a similar lifestyle to his, and who his children mostly played with in the street. Being working class was the more important definition of who one was in Rob's eyes. Asked where he would place his "grouping" in that multiracial society, his first reaction was to say "oh well, there you've got me"; then he opted for a class explanation:

Oh well, like a working class. You know, you get the same in those particular groups. They've got the same sort of thing as us. They've got their working groups too. I usually find with most ethnic groups they're usually, they're more of a hard-working style. They try and achieve a bit more than the Australian does. You know, make their lifestyle that little bit better. They seem to work a bit harder, I've found.

He connected with the Italian tradesman in his street who also worked in the public transport system. The Italian families kept chickens and offered his family their spare eggs: it was a working class ethic of helping each other out that he responded to. He did not know the Vietnamese as well as they were quite new to the area, but he had met Asians at work and had gotten along with them. "I have no trouble with them" he said:

They're pretty keen workers. They learn a job, and nothing seems to be too much trouble for them. They seem to wanta please all the time. No, I've never had any trouble, can't say any bad words about 'em. Some of, I know some of 'em, you can get the good and the bad in every race. The ones we've got are pretty, you know, honest and you know hardworking.

Asked whether he felt there were any "racial groupings" that were overrepresented in Australian society, he believed that the balance was right. "We've got a good sprinkling of everything" he commented, which had "made the country terrific." Australia now had a "big broad lifestyle" where he could sample different traditions and lifestyles. It did not bother him that Greeks or Italians might predominate in some areas. Quite the opposite, it just helped to "make the country different."

What was striking about Rob was his lack of fear about living and working in the midst of ethnic diversity. The working-class suburb that he described as a thriving mix of different peoples was far from the embattled "frontline" suburbs depicted by Blainey (1984) just a few years earlier.

It is a truism of contemporary globalization that more and more nation-states are confronting the dilemmas of multiculturalism, ethnic diversity, and cosmopolitan identity. Population flows have been a major contributing factor, although the relative impact has been contested, with some people arguing that the flows were greater during the nineteenth century (Faist 2000; Held and McGrew 2002: 120). Multiculturalism, some have argued, is less a reaction to increased cultural and ethnic diversity within any given city or nation — many places have exhibited forms of diversity in the past — than the result of the emergence of a new form of political imaginary that recognizes cultural diversity (Kahn 1995: 106–108). Seyla Benhabib has characterized this as a shift in many western capitalist democracies between a politics of redistribution to a politics of recognition, or to a politics of identity. Inspired by various social movements of the 1970s and 1980s, the politics of identity is an expression of "post-materialist values ... signaling a shift from issues of distribution to a concern with the 'grammar' of forms of life..." (Benhabib 1999: 293–294), a trend Benhabib views with considerable skepticism.

Although intellectuals contributed to the adoption of multicultural policy in Australia, the adoption and reception of a multicultural political imaginary has, no doubt, been influenced by the dramatic transformation of the population after the Second World War, from one that was relatively ethnically homogeneous to one that is becoming progressively ethnically diverse. Australia is an immigrant nation, and its destiny has been shaped not only by the determination of its people and governing bodies, but by global trends in political ideology, conflict, and population flow. For the first 150 years of settlement, Anglo-Celtic Australians had very little experience of non-British ethnic concentrations of population (Jupp et al. 1990). There were exceptions. First, they had to deal with indigenous peoples, although their numbers declined rapidly over the course of the nineteenth century (see Chapter Four). There were also small multiracial communities in Australia's far north, involved in the fishing, pearling and sugar industries (Reynolds 2003). South Australia had a relatively large German population, although these people generally blended in with everyone else. Major cities had small Chinese concentrations of population, and visible Chinatowns.

Most immigrants to Australia until the 1940s were of British and Irish descent. Governments through a range of policies (i.e., assisted passages) and restrictions (i.e., Immigration

Restriction Acts) were determined to create in Australia a white British society and a white British population. Up until the end of the Second World War, they were very successful in this endeavor. The Australian experience, with its continuous tradition of strong state control over immigration, can be contrasted with the relatively *laissez-faire* experience and approach of other settler societies such as the United States, Argentina, and Canada, or even older nations like Britain (Jupp 2002: 5–20).

The mass immigration program beginning in 1947 and continuing into the present, stimulated by invasion fears after the Second World War, perceptions of Australia as underpopulated, and by the need to build Australia's "full-employment economy," has progressively transformed Australia's postwar ethnic makeup. Determined to rapidly expand its population, government officials soon found that they could not attract enough Britons to reach the targets, but had to look elsewhere for alternative white immigrants. This competition for immigrants only intensified as the century wore on.

The gradual shift to nondiscriminatory immigration after governments modified the White Australia Policy from the mid-1950s (officially abandoning it in 1973) enhanced this process of ethnic diversification. As analysts of Australia's immigration policies have argued, Australia's reluctant and gradual dismantling of its White Australia Policy came about because of its growing economic and military enmeshment in the Asia-Pacific region, and due to the changing international climate, including decolonization, the consequent rise of new nonwestern nation-states, and the emergence of Japan as a major economic power. Australia could not risk alienating important military and trading partners, and sources for tourism and investment, by continuing to endorse a racist immigration policy (Jupp 1998: chap. 8). Growing interconnectedness, the globalization of economic and political interests, meant that a dearly held nationalist assertion was forced on to the back-foot, and then into retreat.

In the period between 1947 and 1972, Australia's population almost doubled, from seven-and-a-half to thirteen million. More than half of that growth was due to migrants and their Australian-born children (Betts 1988: 2). Since then Australia has gained another six million people, and again immigration has contributed to more than half of this growth. Though initially much of this was British migration, and even in the 1960s almost half of the migrants were British or Irish (Australian Bureau of Statistics 2002), increasingly the trend was to draw upon migrants from Northern and then Southern Europe, with significant numbers from the 1950s coming from Greece and Italy. From the 1970s, immigration from various Asian countries (often English speakers) increased. After the first Indo-Chinese refugees arrived in boats on Australia's northern coasts around 1976 to 1977, Australia's Indo-Chinese communities grew, especially through the family reunion category of immigration policy. By the middle of the 1980s, immigrants from Asia made up 40 to 50 percent of the annual intake (Castles and Miller 1998: 190). This reflected the growing importance of proximity for immigration, once Australian governments ended government-to-government agreements and immigration assistance in the early 1980s. In addition, improvements in the living conditions in European countries made emigration to Australia less attractive to Europeans (Jupp 1998: 120–122). Significant numbers of Lebanese arrived in the 1960s and 1970s, and since then people from many different cultures and backgrounds have been migrating to Australia. Although people of Anglo-Celtic ethnic background still dominate Australia's ethnic makeup, one in five Australians "are not of significantly British or Irish descent, and about one in twenty are not of European descent" (Jupp 1998: 151). Where more than 90 percent of the population before the Second World War was of British or Irish descent and the rest mainly European (Parkin and Hardcastle 1997: 489; Lack and Templeton 1995: xv), there are now significant other European and non-European ethnic groupings in Australia.

An important feature of Australia's ethnic diversity and of its experience of multiculturalism is that, unlike other western countries like the US or Britain, Australia has not seen the emergence of large ethnically defined areas. To the extent that areas of ethnic difference have developed, these tend to contain people from many different ethnic backgrounds, reflecting the diverse sources of Australia's immigration.

Historically, and as with many other countries including the U.S., the main way of understanding how immigrants would relate to Australian society was assimilation. It was assumed that Australia was producing a unified culture and that all immigrants would, and should, desire to adapt to that mainstream culture, leaving much of their own culture and tradition, and their languages, behind. When migration was predominantly British, the overlap between British and Australian identity meant that assimilation was relatively easy and assured. In the postwar period, government sponsored programs like the "Good Neighbor" scheme of the 1950s and 1960s, and integration through work and standard education were meant to help immigrants to make the necessary adaptation. The remnants of "ethnic" cultures and languages were to be restricted for the most part to the private sphere.

This approach began to change during the 1970s when Australia, along with Canada, was one of the first countries to officially embrace multiculturalism as an ethic, and as integral to its national identity (Jupp 1998; Martin 1978; Lopez 2000). The pressure to change came from representatives of non-British immigrant communities and from some policy-makers, academics, and other professionals who believed that there existed in Australian society forms of ethnic disadvantage and discrimination based on the nonrecognition of ethnic cultures and traditions under concepts of assimilation. Assimilation, many argued, had failed, and had inflicted unnecessary suffering on members of Australia's ethnically diverse population. Australia needed a new ethic to unite it as a country and prevent the hemorrhaging of its recent immigrants back to their places of origin.

During the 1970s, the Labor government of Gough Whitlam (1972 to 1975) and the Liberal-National government of Malcolm Fraser (1975 to 1983) articulated a multicultural vision for Australia. After major government reports such as Galbally's 1978 *Migrant Services and Programs: Report of the Review of Post-Arrival Programs and Services for Migrants*, governments at the federal, state, and local levels instituted multicultural public policies (Australia, Review of Post-Arrival Programs and Services for Migrants 1978). During this period the major political parties adopted a bipartisan position accepting nondiscriminatory immigration, repudiating assimilationism, and celebrating Australia's newly emergent ethnic diversity. This also included varying levels of support for the retention of ethnic cultural identities, provided by local, state, and federal governments. From the 1970s, ethnic community councils emerged at the state level, receiving some public funding. The Federation of Ethnic Communities' Councils of Australia, formed in 1979, became the preeminent national representative of ethnic views with access to government, and has received varying levels of government funding since. It has been an important supporter of multiculturalism and this continued support has been "essential," one commentator has argued, "in sustaining government commitment" to the policy (Jupp 1998: 140). One of the most visible forms of public support for ethnic diversity has been the government funding of the Special Broadcasting Service (SBS), which provides multicultural television and radio.

Australia has had, nevertheless, an uneasy relationship with the concept of multiculturalism, despite the official stamp and the optimistic celebration of diversity and harmony among its advocates. Although the evidence from opinion polling is mixed and difficult to interpret, it is fair to say that multiculturalism has never been overwhelmingly endorsed by the general Australian public, even when political leaders were less equivocal in their support for it during the 1970s and early 1980s (Committee to Advise on Australia's Immigration Policies 1988: 30–31; Goot 1988; Markus 1988; Betts 1988: chap. 5). On the other hand, "multiculturalism" can mean many different things and it is not clear from such polls exactly what people support and oppose under that label.

Since the early 1980s, there has been much public debate on multiculturalism and Australian national identity. Although the bipartisan position on multiculturalism was held during the 1970s, it began to break down after the fall of the Fraser government in 1983. While the Labor governments of Bob Hawke (1983 to 1991) and Paul Keating (1991 to 1996) continued to support it, the Liberal and National parties in opposition, and under several leaders, began to distance themselves from, and even openly attack, multiculturalism. This attack was part of a more general conservative critique of multiculturalism that gained considerable momentum in intellectual journals and the popular press and other media after the intervention of the historian Geoffrey Blainey in 1984 (Blainey 1984; Campbell and Uhlmann 1995; for an account of this shift, see Jupp 2002: chap. 6). Under the Liberal–National government of John Howard (1996–), there has been a retreat from the celebration of multiculturalism, although after toying with dropping the term altogether, it has more recently accepted the value of its continued public use.

Immigration: A Commitment to Australia, the important government report on Australia's immigration policies published in 1988, although not itself an attack on multiculturalism, suggested that the term elicited a hostile response from the general public, and implied that its public use might be counterproductive in efforts to gain public support for Australia's nondiscriminatory immigration program (Committee to Advise on Australia's Immigration Policies 1988: chap. 4 and *passim*). The Hawke government's subsequent *National Agenda for a Multicultural Australia: Sharing Our Future* explicitly denied any link between multicultural and immigration policies, and stressed that multiculturalism was a "policy for managing the consequences of cultural diversity," not for creating it. The limits to multiculturalism were also stressed, with the assertion that multicultural policies were "based upon the premise that all Australians should have an overriding and unifying commitment to Australia, to its interests and future first and foremost." Individuals had the right to maintain and develop their cultural traditions, but "within carefully defined limits," and while respecting all other identities and traditions (Department of the Prime Minister and Cabinet, Office of Multicultural Affairs 1989: vii):

> Multicultural policies require all Australians to accept the basic
> structures and principles of Australian society — the
> Constitution and the rule of law, tolerance and equality,
> Parliamentary democracy, freedom of speech and religion,
> English as the national language and equality of the sexes.

This was not a commitment to separate cultures living side-by-side, but to a cohesive, diverse Australian nation in which all had an equal stake.

Despite these limits, and despite the fact that Australia was not made up of segregated ethnic communities, the conservative intellectuals' attack on multiculturalism was vigorous during the 1980s and 1990s. It seemed, as Jupp (2002) has argued, to transplant criticism coming out of the U.S. and its very different history and experience onto the Australian situation (for an account of the American experience, see Glazer 1997 and Schlesinger Jr. 1992). Rather than characterize the complex detail of that debate, or for that matter discuss the nature of ongoing intellectual support for multiculturalism, I want to clarify the main forms of critique of multiculturalism that have emerged among Australian commentators. While there has been a minor left critique of multiculturalism, arguing, for example, that it is an ideology that obscures the important class cleavages of Australian society and undermines working class solidarity, that it has promoted middle-class elites as unelected spokespersons for ethnic groups, and even that it is an ideology concealing ongoing forms of "white" or

"Anglo" privilege and control of national space (i.e., see Hage 1998), I will leave this to one side and concentrate on the more visible forms of public critique from the right.

The first can be thought of as a matter of culture, history, and national pride. The critique operates, in other words, at the level of "culture wars." Here the argument is that so-called "multiculturalists" are anti-Australian culture, or more precisely "anti" the British heritage of Australian culture. It is claimed that multiculturalists want to "rewrite Australian history," and that they insult Australian nationality.

Second, there is the straightforward argument about government spending. Some critics claim that governments should not spend any money on programs that help ethnic groups maintain their languages, cultures, and traditions. This argument is misplaced, according to Jupp (2002). The adoption of multicultural policy in Australia was driven by a need to allocate funds in such a way that previously excluded sections of the Australian community could now participate fully in Australian society. Given the assimilationist strand in Australian political culture, if governments were seen as promoting ethnic separatism, this would prove a powerful argument against multicultural policy. But multicultural public policy has largely meant settlement and integration policy, not support for the maintenance of cultural difference. Funding could range from practical measures like making sure that public information was available in a variety of languages besides English, and/or providing translators, that services (especially in the areas of education, health, and social welfare) were culturally sensitive so that all cultures could equally enjoy them (these might include services run by ethnic communities), to programs such as funding to already existing ethnic organizations for cultural activities and so on (Jupp 2002: chap. 5). It has included some funding for the retention of languages (i.e., through support for ethnic language schools on weekends, and for teaching community languages in the public education system) and subsidizing religious schools (Jupp 1998: chap. 9). The strong claim from critics about this sort of government approach and spending is that it promotes separatism and impedes assimilation into mainstream culture, and, moreover, that it is an unnecessary burden on the government purse (Campbell and Uhlmann 1995).

A third criticism is that any government promotion of the ideal of multiculturalism, regardless of financial considerations, is a fatal step for Australia. Governments, in other words, should not be seen to support notions of cultural diversity. Rather, they should be seen to actively promote the idea that Australia is a single nation with shared values and traditions, and that people living here should adapt to that strong sense of a unified culture. The assumption among these critics seems to be that Australia's cultural diversity is only maintained because governments and intellectuals promote it. Rather than seeing government celebration of multiculturalism as an inclusive gesture recognizing that Australia has, in fact, become far more culturally and ethnically diverse, these critics see government and intellectuals as "creating" a divided, multicultural society with an increasingly fragmenting sense of identity. This is to say, such critics appear to operate under the belief that problems of cultural diversity and cultural tension would disappear if governments stopped "promoting" diversity.

Extending such critique, Blainey, among others, warned of the potential danger of the development of "warring tribes" within the nation-state, as witnessed in various multiethnic countries around the world, should Australian governments continue to promote and pursue multicultural policies (Blainey 1984: 170–171, 1991: 48, 140, 1994: 233). Such warnings have been made in the relative absence of ethnic conflict on Australian streets (Holton 1991). More controversially, in 1984 Blainey sparked a major race debate after commenting in a speech at a regional center that the level of Asian immigration ought to be slowed down in the interests of social cohesion, comments he backed up with a book-length polemic (Blainey 1984). In 1988, John Howard, at that time Opposition leader, made the following comments on radio, reigniting debate about Australia's future:

> I believe that Asian migration is in the eyes of some of the community too great; it would be in our immediate-term interests in terms of social cohesion if we could slow down a little so that the capacity of the community to absorb this would become greater (cited in Cope and Kalantzis 2000: 195).

The context for these criticisms was the Hawke government's attempt, during the 1980s, to articulate a cosmopolitan Australian identity and to move the nation further away from its old image as a white Australia. Moreover, the Hawke government and even more vigorously the Keating government of the 1990s emphasized Australia's greater involvement in the Asia-Pacific region. These governments stressed that unlike in the past when Australia sought to secure itself *against* the threat of Asia — both militarily, and in terms of national identity — Australians of the present would seek to secure their future in the Asia-Pacific region, and *with* the people and countries of the region. Australians would continue to feel much more at ease with Asia and the links would grow deeper with time. Australia's own growing Asian population would assist in forging these economic and cultural links.

The backlash against this position gained some momentum in the 1990s when Pauline Hanson, a maverick former endorsed candidate for the Liberal Party, became an independent MP and started her own populist party One Nation, which, among other things, called for the dismantling of multiculturalism and for a halt to the "Asianization" of Australia. At the height of her success and notoriety in the late 1990s, her party gathered about one million votes across Australia.

The public debate over multiculturalism and its meanings, and the attempts to limit its horizons by, for example, emphasizing the primacy of national identification, highlight problems that nation-states, including immigrant nations like Australia, have with handling diversity within their own boundaries. Most nationalisms have entailed notions of homogeneity of population. Ernest Gellner (1983), although no ardent nationalist himself, saw cultural homogeneity, and its honoring, as integral to nationalism, and as stemming from the great social changes that underpinned the rise of nation-states and nationalism. One of the necessary conditions of existence of the industrial age, as an age of perpetual "growth" societies, was a mobile, creative citizenry capable of producing, understanding, and responding to context-free forms of communication (Gellner 1987: 14–15). "The need for cultural homogeneity," Gellner argued, "follows from the requirements of rapid, easy and precise communication, of the possibility of slotting people into new economic roles, of a complex, sophisticated, and quickly changing division of labor" (Gellner 1987: 113). Nations, according to most nationalists, need basic agreements on values, including political values. Some nationalists go further, claiming that members of nations need to be animated by the same ideals, and that they must be able to communicate and mix with each other freely, not just sharing a common language, but a shared way of thinking and feeling, rooted in a shared history. For some, this must be rooted in common ethnic belonging, while for others it should, at the very least, be the stated aim of the society's leaders and institutions. As such, diversity, except for individual diversity, has always been a problem for nationalism.

But what of the *particular* Australian dream of homogeneity? Important here is Australia's historical development as an overwhelmingly British society, its long adherence to "white Australia" nationalism, and the way that Australians saw their egalitarianism and ethnocultural homogeneity as inextricably linked. Like other settler societies, Australian society was animated by the ideology of newness, pitting itself against the Old World. But the contrast between "old" and "new" was selective, and it was never simply a case of opting for the "new" against the "old." Australia saw itself, for example, as a British society following British values, and in some respects, outdoing Britain in its Britishness. At the same time, it saw itself as free of the stultifying traditions, and the class hierarchies, of the Old World that included Britain. Australia's nationalist vision was animated not only by the desire to avoid the problems of the Old World, but by a desire to avoid the "racial" problems that beset New World societies like the United States and Southern Africa.

What did the notions of homogeneity promise to Australians? By keeping the society British, the belief was that Australia could achieve and maintain an egalitarian society where everyone lived a decent life and would head in the one progressive direction. There would be no room for exploitation by race, color, or caste. Because everyone would expect the same out of life, there would be no room for undercutting working men's wages and conditions. The country would be free of the racial conflicts that marred other countries, and the "crimson thread of kinship," in other words shared British blood, would unite and keep all together, despite differences of opinion, belief, and station. One could look into the eyes of other citizens on the street, wherever one went in Australia, and understand them. That, at least, was the powerful and prevailing fantasy.

Habermas has argued that in a globalizing world where the ethnic composition of most nation-states is "changing under the pressure of waves of global migration" (1994: 128), nation-states can no longer rely for their cohesion upon "a substantive consensus on values," let alone upon common ethnic ties of loyalty and understanding. Instead, states must rely upon "a consensus on the procedures for the legitimate enactment of laws and the legitimate exercise of power" (1994: 135). The preconditions for stable constitutional states include a broad agreement among citizens on a single political culture under which those different forms of life might prosper and proliferate. Habermas argues that different cultural forms of life can and do coexist within unified states, and that states, or more precisely governments, should not demand more cultural conformity than is strictly necessary under the banner of a common and limited political culture. This, argues Habermas, is the unavoidable condition of a globalizing world (see also Habermas 2001).

This multicultural solution to the question of national identity and citizenship in complex modern societies may not, however, convince the critics of Australian multiculturalism who, it would appear, view nostalgically Australia's experience of British homogeneity. Many such critics remain hopeful for a return to strong agreement on "Australian" values and a single way of life rather than the complex of different forms of life that now coexist, sometimes peacefully, at other times conflictually, in so many nation-states, including Australia, today.

Given Australia's history of Britishness, and the commitment to such a style of community as the bedrock of Australian identity and national cohesion, even fostering and contributing to egalitarian ideals, and given the ethnic transformation of the Australian population since the Second World War, it is hardly surprising that the question of ethnic diversity has been surrounded by controversy. It is also less than surprising that many of the figures (although not all of them) at the forefront of Australian conceptualization of multiculturalism and multicultural policies were from non-Anglo-Celtic Australian backgrounds (Lopez 2000). It has been argued by some that Anglo-Celtic Australians, who had largely failed to even recognize their indigenous peoples, had no real traditions for dealing with or understanding ethnic diversity. These, so the argument goes, had to be invented, and evidence of such invention can be found in new expressions of nationalism such as that contained in the multicultural notion of "unity through diversity."

However, Australia's homogeneity of population before the Second World War should not be exaggerated. There has been a tendency to look back at the old white Australia in a way that treats as insignificant what were, in reality, serious rifts and differences, as if Australians in the past did not have to work hard to maintain social cohesion and harmony. Class differences in

Australia were very important for a large swathe of that history, with strong, urban working-class communities living apart from more affluent middle- and upper-class communities, almost inhabiting different worlds. "Britishness" itself contained considerable ethnic and religious differences, often intertwining and reinforcing each other — the Catholic/Protestant division of the society fed through Irish, English, Scottish, and Welsh identities. This was remarked upon by people like Alan, as I showed above. Kel (the shearer discussed earlier), looking back to the history of his own small rural town, also claimed that Australia had, from its beginnings, always been multicultural:

I've grown up in there and we've been a multicultural town since it was first settled in 1870. You've only got to read the history of the town and read about the Irish and the Scottish people. And the Irish people lived up one end of the town and the Scottish people lived up the other end of the town, and all the Germans and Chinese, they all lived in the middle of town. So it was a multicultural place back then. I mean when we were first settled it was multicultural then because you had English convicts, you had Aboriginals and you had the Irish and you had the Pommies [Australian slang for the English] who were running the show, and you always hear about Americans coming over here back in the early days. So I mean we've been multicultural since day one.

Some historians have argued that because Anglo-Celtic Australia had to confront the issue of ethnic diversity in the past, even if on a more limited scale than is evident today, Australian political culture had already developed the capacity to handle diversity, long before the mass migrations after the Second World War. Australians had found ways to accommodate and defuse ethnic and religious differences at the public culture level by separating church from state, ensuring public recognition of religious equality, and by providing nonreligious public education. It is these capacities, especially for tolerance, it has been argued, that Australians drew upon to maintain a cohesive society as the population became more ethnically diverse in the late twentieth century (see Hirst 1995, 2002).

Tolerance, however, is not the same as celebration and embracing of diversity. Tolerance more often meant conveniently ignoring difference, or underplaying its relevance for Australian life. If the capacity for tolerance existed in the more ethnically homogeneous pre-Second World War Australia, it was perhaps the experience of living with the benefits of diversity brought by postwar immigration that unleashed the multicultural imagination. The infusion of new ideas, foods, languages and diverse cultural life — a largely unintended effect of the immigration program (Lack and Templeton 1995) — and the capacities brought to the society by postwar immigrants themselves, gradually, over the decades, allowed for multicultural celebration.

The ability of the Australian population to find creative ways to understand and handle its ethnic and cultural diversity was apparent in many of the interviews collected by our research team in the late 1980s, and in the present. From this vantage point, the more combative and alarmist assertions about multiculturalism, often honed for public consumption and in pursuit of a political agenda, are not necessarily reflective of experiences on the ground, as it were, even among the "old" Anglo-Celtic Australians. Where such concerns do arise, they may find more reflective and nuanced expression.

The reality of living in an increasingly multicultural society, quite apart from the clamor of voices for and against "multiculturalism," has important implications for everyday life, and for feelings and expressions of nationhood. Most commented upon by people with any experience of pre- or early post-Second World War Australian society, are the different foods, the different languages spoken in public spaces, and the many different appearances of people on Australian streets. Some streets are noticeably "ethnic," with signs and advertising in languages other than English.

Katerina, the young Greek Australian teacher introduced in the previous chapter, celebrated this everyday experience of multiculturalism. Multiculturalism was for her simply what she experienced as she went about her daily life, teaching at her private school, walking along the street and seeing people of varying ethnic backgrounds, or going into a corner shop where she was served by a Chinese man. Looking around at the people and the life of her own city, she sensed a sort of cosmopolitanism gradually taking hold. Asked what a cosmopolitan society would be like, she said:

> My view would be a large or a fairly extensive tapestry of people. This tapestry of people would encompass different races, different colors, different creeds, different religious backgrounds, and a different mix within society of, perhaps, old, young, middle of the road. I suppose "cosmopolitan" has the feel of it being a little bit more racier in terms of, you know, things that aren't stagnant, it's moving always and things are changing to an extent.

Katerina embraced and celebrated change and movement. Where for some people flux and change bring bewilderment, and even mourning for a past that is lost, this constant movement made for interest and excitement in her view. Where for others the differences that she highlights and enthuses over brought confusion and fear, there was little evidence of these feelings bothering Katerina. Even so, she recognized the potential conflicts, and that there could be tensions between groups brought to Australia:

> When we have more than one person living within an area of course you're going to have conflicts. I suppose with different groups of people living within the one area under the same rules and under the same society, you will have conflicts … Perhaps what one group of people wants is not the same as what another group wants. That will bring a flare in society, a disagreement and perhaps a change for the better, but sometimes it won't, sometimes it will cause disagreements and tension. I think that many of the ethnic groups that do come over to Australia, while bringing in a culture and different types of lifestyles, like food, music or whatever, they can also bring with them tensions from that particular society.

Katerina was referring to the conflict between the Macedonians and Greeks that had recently flared up, and the problems in Yugoslavia more generally, and the way that when these conflicts were brought to Australia it created an uneasy tension even for those not directly involved. The feeling, that she had heard expressed by people around her, was "why do they bring their problems here?" But she was not certain that this was the right attitude. "It's not always easy" she pointed out, to leave behind the problems that immigrants and refugees are escaping from. It was not so simple as people made it seem when they said: "If they are going to be part of our culture, then let them be part of our culture, they can be Australian, let them forget about their problems back there."

Australians had to make the best of it in the hope that these things would iron themselves out in the long run, said Katerina. Making the best of it meant searching for the "right balance" between ethnic pride and belonging to a country that contained people from many different ethnic backgrounds. Katerina was against exclusivism: multiculturalism was for her an ethic of tolerance and acceptance, of maintaining one's heritage while at the same time engaging with, and actively enjoying, the wider society. In other words, there was a common society even if there was not a common culture, in any strong sense of the term.

In this new kind of complex Australia, where diversity is inside and not just outside the nation, people must manage a range of fears and complexities, and in many cases operate with a more complicated map of society than, perhaps, was previously required. Many people live with the feeling, or the suspicion, that they no longer inhabit a place of complete familiarity. They must live with the fact that there are small pockets of ethnic "strangeness" to which they have little or no real or imaginative access. Leaders and commentators may feel less sure that they can speak for all Australians, rather than merely for some sections of Australian society, in a public voice that assumes that the types of communication and general understanding are shared. Sometimes there are public explosions of suspicion about ethnically marked groups, such as "Asians," and increasingly the ethnically heterogeneous but homogenized "Muslims," particularly around issues of supposed gang behavior and crime.

Australian national identity, as I suggested in the last chapter, has become more complicated, even multifaceted. There is, moreover, the spectre of multiple loyalties. Many Australians had always exhibited dual loyalties. The hyphenated British-Australian, or even the Irish Catholic-Australian, came long before any notion of other hyphenated Australians. And yet, the dual loyalties have proliferated, and in some cases become even more complex, multinational, loyalties. (I am thinking here, but not only, of Muslim identities.) This is troubling for some people, as evident in this recent exchange with Wayne, the mechanic first interviewed in the late 1980s, now in his forties:

> They [Muslims in Australia] can't be patriotic because their religion says they can't. [*They don't think they can be as loyal to Australia as anyone else?*] Well they wouldn't be because the king Muslim, whoever he is, if Allah says you will kill Australians, well he comes first. Religion comes before anything in the world for those that believe it. So if they're a naturalized Australian, they may have a business where they wear Australian jumpers and make Australian flags all day long and they run in the Olympics, but then if the religion side of it says you will kill all Australians, they will do it. Because they're brainwashed to it. That's where their patriotism is, to their religion.

Diasporic communities do not necessarily maintain loyalty to one country, but develop and maintain other forms of transnational identity. In the main, however, these do not take the extremist form feared by Wayne. Nor is this an issue peculiar to Australia. It is a feature of the globalizing world, aided not simply by multicultural policies, but by a range of developments, some of the most important being in the areas of transport and communications (Anderson 1998; Cohen 1997).

People like Katerina and Rosa fully embraced the promise of multicultural identity. Multiculturalism, in this sense, does not mean the death of national identity, but it does mean its realignment. It is often and incorrectly assumed by nationalist critics of multiculturalism that maintaining a strong sense of ethnic identity is somehow opposed to having a sense of Australian nationhood. Why should we imagine that it is not perfectly conceivable that, in this global age, one could be, say, proudly Greek and proudly Australian, as if the two were mutually exclusive? Innumerable examples of proud ethnic identity coupled with proud Australianness among Australia's major ethnic groupings suggest otherwise.

Pham, a Vietnamese refugee who has made a life for himself in Australia since the early 1980s, when asked about his identity said the following:

I see myself as an Australian from a Vietnamese background. When I say "we" I really mean it. Yeah, I put myself in, I'm talking about history and we in Australia at that time we didn't want them [single Vietnamese men], things like that, yeah.

He was talking about his own initial difficulties as a single Vietnamese immigrant in the early 1980s. From the vantage point of 2003, he could put himself into Australian history as a member of the national "we," even before he entered the society, because he was now Australian and felt that he had the right to speak about Australia, its traditions, and its history as an insider. At the same time, he was an elder in a Vietnamese family "clan" with a strong interest in Vietnam and Vietnamese culture, and in Vietnamese associations and welfare in Australia. "I'm a living example," he said "of the success of the multicultural ... of multicultural policy."

Given the travel opportunities these days, many sons and daughters of immigrants returning to their parents' former homelands are, like Katerina, confirmed in their understanding that they are Australians. Multiculturalism, importantly, gives people from Australia's many different ethnic backgrounds, who do not necessarily have the long generational association with Australia so important for many Anglo-Celtic Australians, a point of identification with the nation. People like Rosa, Katerina, and Pham have a clear stake in seeing Australia as a multicultural society. It gives them a sense of efficacy and ownership of at least some aspects of the national identity in a context where people from their immigrant backgrounds have been on many occasions excluded, or encouraged to remain silent, in the past. A generous view of multiculturalism (like Rosa's) would point out that it is not promoting separatism, but rather social inclusion and a new unity responding to the ethnic transformation of the Australian polity.

Tjaart was asked back in 1988 what his thoughts were about the situation for Aborigines in contemporary Australian society. He was confident and forthright in his opinions, which were based on almost no personal contact with Aborigines:

> My view is that some of them will come into our society or they'll become part of our society and they'll become western-ized the same as most of the rest of us are and there are others who won't. And the ones who don't will, in the longer term, just be drowned out or perish or whatever, but just be left behind.

When asked how he felt about that, he replied that he still felt "reasonably comfortable about it," a comfort that was based on an interpretation of the vast sweep of history with its many invasions and destructions of whole peoples, cultures, and ways of life. As I noted in a previous chapter, by 2002 Tjaart's views had softened, and this was also true for the way that he felt about the Aboriginal situation. During the 15 years between the first and second interviews, he had traveled to Australia's center and north, and what he had seen, including the poverty, violence, and social disorder, had affected him profoundly:

> There are groups of people like, whatever, Pauline Hanson, who says that the Aboriginals are just leeches on our system. I

don't accept that for one minute. What I saw in Alice Springs was two groups of people living in totally, absolutely totally different worlds, but actually living in the same space. Just totally different worlds. And I suspect that it's going to take a long time. Time is the only thing that's going to do anything to change that. Throwing money at it I don't think's going to work. … Another group says let them live the way they want to live. There's another group of them that wants to put them all in houses and make them [live] the way we live. I can tell you that doesn't work. … So there is the issue, again we're talking about revolution and casualties of war. These people are major casualties of all these changes. Their background may be educated, may not be educated, but their way of living in the community that they find themselves in, they have great, great difficulty.

When nonindigenous Australians try to grapple with and understand the plight of Australia's indigenous people today, the intellectual and moral resources they bring to that confrontation rarely seem up to the task. I do not say this with any sense of superiority — as a settler Australian I also find myself struggling with what is a historical fate — but in recognition of the real difficulties that the history of colonization imposes upon all of us, indigenous and nonindigenous alike. This is not to suggest that the difficulties are of the same intensity and magnitude for the two groups. While nonindigenous Australians experience discomfort, indigenous Australians suffer intensely, both physically and emotionally, as a result of ongoing colonization.

Take, for example, the issue of Aboriginal land rights. How vividly I remember discussing the concept with undergraduate students during the early 1990s. Repeatedly in the different classes, one or more students would utter the same refrain about lands that had some form of Aboriginal claim over them: it was not right that they, as Australians, should have to seek permission from Aboriginal owners or custodians in order to enter and use "Australian" land. Karen, a young mother and tertiary student when interviewed in the late 1980s, explained her own ambivalent feelings about land rights:

I can remember years ago first going into the Northern Territory [...] and coming to a fence and not being allowed to go on that land unless you had a permit to go on there, and thinking, you know, "This is my country; why can't *I* go where *I* want within it?" and getting angry then. But then again, it is *their* land. Yeah, that's a really hard one because where do you draw the line, I suppose? At the moment I'm still in favor of it, but then to get the assemblies of the tribes asking for Melbourne back or ... At the moment you know, the Aboriginals are just claiming land in Northern Australia. That's a hard one. [...] Overall I'd have to say yes, I was in favor of it. But like anything there's two sides to the argument.

Don, the semiretired doctor discussed in earlier chapters, so liberal in his views about many things, so open in his willingness to embrace many types of Australians from many different backgrounds, and so supportive of the underdog, found a stumbling block in the concept of Aboriginal land rights. He simply could not reconcile it with his beliefs about egalitarianism:

... why should I support land rights? Every little bit or plot of ground that I own, my brother owns, my family own, and so forth, was all achieved by simple hard work and endeavor and people should only own possessions or, not possessions I suppose; basically as human beings we're entitled to certain possessions like food, clothing, health, but other possessions are things that should be worked for and appreciated.

While he accepted that Aborigines had a legitimate grievance, he was at the limit of his wits to know what might be fairly done about it.

Olga, the daughter of post-Second World War Ukranian immigrants, lived on a farm in an area that had experienced recent controversy over sacred sites and a native title claim. Interviewed in 2003, she could not understand what all the fuss was about with land rights: "Everybody came out here and they bought up the land, and so there was nothing stopping the Aboriginals doing the same either, was there?" She suspected that Aborigines were making bogus claims: "Well I just think it's one way of getting a financial thing. It's only just talk and it makes you think 'why there? Why not here?'"

There are, of course, more positive views, but large sections of the Australian public remain skeptical, or against either Aboriginal land rights as they already exist, or any further extension of them (see Australian National Opinion Polls 1985; Irving Saulwick and Associates 2000: 36). It is still difficult for many Australians of non-Aboriginal descent to appreciate that Aborigines might have special claims upon the land that do not fit in with European or contemporary "Australian" notions of the way that one acquires and deals with land. On the other hand, the difficulty is also rooted in notions of Australian egalitarianism — "all Australians should be treated equally," "no special treatment" — and in the very concepts and experience of nationalism and nationhood. To have nationality means that one has a relationship with national space, with national territory. Within that national territory, there are, of course, many areas, like fenced-off private property, military facilities, and so on, that one cannot enter at will. Nevertheless, the assumption is that all nationals, who have the same form of claim and inheritance, enjoy the national territory, more or less equally. Aboriginal relationships with Australian land complicate this neat national picture. The difficulty is also related to the meaning and significance of Australian places for, and to feelings of belonging and identity among, the people of many different backgrounds in Australia (Read 2000).

The great European expansion beginning in the late fifteenth century fundamentally reshaped the world. It has involved the massive shifting of products and people around the globe, the transformation of ancient societies and civilizations, and the setting up of new settler societies in the Americas, Southern Africa, and Australasia. It brought vastly different peoples and their cultures together, and resulted in ongoing interactions between those peoples and cultures.

George M. Fredrickson (1988), the comparative historian of racism, classifies the varying colonial situations found across the globe under four major categories: "occupation," "mixed settlement," "plantation," and "pure settlement."[1] During the age of expansion, European colonizers exploited many of the more densely populated and organized societies of Africa and South East Asia for labor and material goods, and used them as a market for surplus European goods. In these colonies of occupation, the primary aim (and opportunity) was thus not to settle European populations (although this usually occurred to some extent), nor to impose a European political and legal framework over the territory and its indigenous populations (although again this happened to a lesser or greater extent). As Fredrickson points out, "the new European overlords could profit most handily by skimming a surplus 'off the top' without systematically destroying the traditional cultures, modes of production, or forms of local governance." As a consequence, these colonies "did not undergo a radical and thoroughgoing social reorganization to reflect the hegemony of a substantial and permanent white status group" (1988: 219). In the colonies of settlement (i.e., the other three categories), on the other hand, European colonizers primarily sought the land itself, and not indigenous labor or goods, for exploitation and to provide space for surplus European population. In societies like South Africa and America (hybrids of the plantation and mixed settlement types), the Latin American countries (mixed settlement), the sugar islands of the West Indies (plantation), and Australia (pure settlement), the attempt was to set up European style societies in new lands, under the assumption that this represented the spread of civilization. Of the three types of settlement colony, Australia stood as the most perfect example, to such a degree that many had been tempted to refer to this ideal type as "the Australian case." The indigenous peoples were, in a sense, almost completely peripheral to the colonizing project, to the imposition of the mode of production from which they were largely excluded.

The long story of globalization in Australia involves the movement from the Aboriginal erasure implied by Fredrickson's notion of pure settlement to the heightened visibility of Aboriginality and Aboriginal claims in the contemporary period. For Australia's Aborigines and Torres Strait Islanders (hereafter referred to together as Australia's Aborigines or indigenous peoples), globalization in its previous and contemporary forms has meant challenges to tradition, the ongoing transformation of tradition, and the reassertion of tradition as a meaningful anchoring for life and society.

From the late eighteenth to the late nineteenth century, globalization was for Australia's Aborigines a largely destructive force, bringing disease, dispossession, dislocation, murder, the decimation of the population, and cultural devastation. At the time of the British invasion, the indigenous population of Australia was divided into hundreds of tribal, subtribal, or clan groupings in tribal areas throughout Australia and its nearby coastal islands. Most Aborigines sustained themselves by hunting and gathering activities, although practices and lifestyles, and degrees of mobility varied considerably in different geographical areas, from the coast to the inland deserts. It is now well-known that indigenous peoples worked extensively to transform the Australian environment to suit their needs, rather than simply roamed over it and fossicked upon it. Firing undergrowth to improve hunting was a common practice. In various parts of Australia, Aborigines used complicated fishing traps and weirs in river systems (Blainey 1985: 139–142), and engaged in horticultural practices (e.g., in Cape York in the northeast of Australia). Peoples like the Torres Strait Islanders in Australia's north led more settled, village-based lifestyles. While some Aborigines built fixed structures, others did not (Lourandos 1997). Cultures, languages, and belief systems were also very diverse, and remain so today.

Estimates of how many Aborigines occupied Australia prior to 1788 vary, from as few as 250,000 to more than 1,000,000

(Lourandos 1997: chap. 2). By the turn of the twentieth century, it was estimated that there were approximately 93,000 surviving Aborigines and it was widely expected that this "remnant" would die off altogether in the not too distant future. The twentieth century, however, saw the slow recuperation of the indigenous population. The latest population figures based on the 2001 Census indicate that there were approximately 460,000 indigenous people in Australia, which accounts for around 2 percent of the Australian population (Australian Bureau of Statistics 2003).

To emphasize the largely destructive nature of this early phase of globalization is not to argue that indigenous peoples, in Australia or elsewhere, were simply its victims. Australia's Aborigines not only resisted but also engaged with these new forces and technologies, adapting and surviving against terrible odds (Broome 1994). From first contact with the British and other Europeans, they found ways to incorporate not only new technologies (metal axes, clothing) and sources of food (flour, sugar, tobacco, sheep, cattle), but also the very presence of white people into their mythic structures and social organization (Reynolds 1987, 1990). They quickly learned to converse in English with colonists, and expressed curiosity in British culture and habits. During the nineteenth century, when they were being confined to missions, stations, and reserves, there were important examples like the farming settlement at Corandeerk in Victoria where, until they were betrayed by colonial governments and by avaricious white settlers, Aborigines proved themselves capable of establishing thriving farming enterprises (Barwick 1972). Where Aborigines were used most extensively for labor, as stockmen and farm laborers on the vast pastoral runs and stations upon which Australia's economic prosperity was built, they proved indispensable. In other words, they were agents involved in the same globalizing forces, even as they were its undoubted victims. Indigenous people's agency and adaptation to the challenges of globalization continue into the present, in increasingly sophisticated forms.

There were different ways of seeing Aborigines within this period, with early images of hard and soft primitivism, or ignoble and noble savagery jostling for position in European imaginations. As Bernard Smith (1969) and others (Mulvaney 1957) have shown, ignoble savagery gained the upper hand during the nineteenth century as the pastoral frontier spread. Smith noted the curious phenomenon that as European reactions to Australia became, after 1820, in general more favorable, reactions to Aborigines became less favorable. In the new Australian Eden, the only debased thing was the savage, predatory, unpredictable Aborigine (Smith 1969: 202–203). This needs to be understood as a dynamic relation. At the time when squatters were pushing out beyond the frontiers of settlement, from the 1820s onward, and meeting with Aboriginal resistance, Aborigines were an obstacle that stood in the way of settler dreams of development and progress. Dispossession needed to be justified. Aborigines became the shocking jest on nature and humanity at exactly the time when a careful consideration of their moral and property rights would have hindered more powerful interests.

To the extent that white settlers needed to explain these actions to themselves — and as moral agents they inevitably had to, at least on some occasions — there was a range of options. First and most important was the claim that, because Aborigines had never "truly" occupied or possessed the land through labor and improvement (i.e., per John Locke's argument), the settlement of Australia did not involve dispossessing them. The international law doctrine legitimizing this ideological notion was *terra nullius*. For some, Aborigines fell to the animal side of the human/animal divide: they had not separated themselves from nature in such a manner that warranted seeing them as human. They seemed to live off nature like ranging animals. Describing his experiences and travels in the English-speaking world during 1866 and 1867, Charles Dilke had this to say about attitudes towards Aborigines:

> Nothing will persuade the rougher class of Queensland settlers that the "black-fellow" and his "jin" are human. They tell you freely that they look upon the native Australian as an ingenious kind of monkey ... (1872: 357).

Such views were not, one might add, restricted to those of the rougher classes. They were not based simply on direct experience, but also upon gossip, anecdote, and upon what could be gathered from travel books, newspaper articles and popular magazines and journals, produced in Britain and in the Australian colonies (Christie 1979: 31).

For others, especially the Christian missionaries and the humanitarians (Reynolds 1998), Aborigines were most definitely human, but they needed to be worked upon and reshaped in order to fit into the order of western Christian civilization. They had to be educated, divested of their "heathen" beliefs, forced to settle down, to become an agricultural people and so on. Those of the first, racist, persuasion looked cynically on the activities and schemes of the Christian missionaries and "Exeter Hall" humanitarians, and saw the failure of their efforts to civilize Aborigines as further evidence of Aboriginal savagery and inherent incapacity (Christie 1979). As the nineteenth century wore on, and under the influence of scientific racism, these negative views of Aborigines hardened.

When the colonies federated in 1901, the belief that Australia's destiny was as a white nation was held almost unanimously across the political factions and across the classes. The notion of a white Australia had emerged in the nineteenth century as a nationalist assertion that included beliefs in racial superiority, but also liberal beliefs about the importance of shared political traditions and beliefs for the functioning of liberal polity. It expressed the straightforward interest of protecting comparatively high wages from sources of cheaper labor. In dealing with and thinking about the bulk of the nonwhite world, this provided a clear-cut understanding. Nonwhites were aliens, they would be kept out by immigration restriction policies, and where they remained within the national territory they would not belong to the nation: they would not receive the same benefits of citizenship, they would be excluded from certain activities, and would not be able to fully participate in the political life of the nation. Examples include the Chinese who arrived in large numbers in the 1850s during Australia's gold rushes, but whose numbers were steadily reduced by such policies, and the Pacific Islanders who had been used for pearling, fishing, and on the sugar plantations, many of whom were deported in the first decade of the twentieth century. This situation, as I explained in the last chapter, only began to break down in the 1950s and 1960s.

Australian Aborigines represented a more complex case. They were not white, and yet, though vastly reduced in numbers, decimated through disease, ill-treatment, incarceration, and discrimination, they existed within the national territory. Since the latter half of the nineteenth century, under the regime of protection, many had been placed in government and church-run missions, stations, and reserves, and thus kept separate from settler Australians, many of whom could thereby conveniently forget about them. Even if anyone had proposed expelling Aborigines from Australia — as had been proposed for other nonwhite "races" — it was not feasible, and certainly not acceptable to British authorities. Nevertheless, to a large extent the same category of *alienness* used for other nonwhites was applied to them. They were not to be counted in the national census (remarkably this was not altered until the constitutional amendments of 1967). For the most part, with some exceptions, they would not be able to vote. But what were Aborigines if they were not Australians? On the other hand, how could they be Australians if they were not white? The debate on the franchise at the Commonwealth level indicates these tensions, with the liberal government of the time forced into amending its proposed legislation so that the 1902 *Commonwealth Franchise Act* "effectively barred Australian Aborigines from the rights of citizenship" (Chesterman and Galligan 1997: 89). Aborigines had voting rights in some colonies before federation, and continued to exercise these rights in some states after federation, but the 1902 *Commonwealth Franchise Act* (in various amended forms), in combination with the activities of bureaucrats, excluded most Aborigines from voting until 1962. Many of the arguments against Aborigines having the vote, especially those emanating from Queensland and Western Australia, were based on racist claims about the capacities and way of living of Aborigines. On the other hand, Richard O'Connor, the government senator responsible for initiating the legislation, was clearly troubled by the exclusion:

[I]t would be a monstrous thing, an unheard of piece of savagery on our part, to treat the aboriginals, whose land we were occupying, in such a manner as to deprive them absolutely of any right to vote in their own country, simply on the ground of their colour, and because they were aboriginals … (quoted in Chesterman and Galligan 1997: 90).

For others, the dilemma of Aborigines within a white nation was handled by pretending that Aborigines simply were not there, or very soon would not be (i.e., they were a "dying race," a myth that extended from the early nineteenth century up to the 1930s [McGregor 1997]). During the long debates on the Immigration Restriction Bill during 1901 and 1902, where politicians discoursed on their hopes and fears for their national community as a white Australia, the glaring absence of the Aborigines from the discussion can be explained not only by the nature of the debate — they were not immigrants who could be restricted — but also by the pervasiveness of this belief that they were doomed. One of the only mentions made of Aborigines was in Attorney General Alfred Deakin's Second Reading Speech on the Bill:

We have power to deal with people of any and every race within our borders, except the aboriginal inhabitants of the continent, who remain under the custody of the States. There is that single exception of a dying race; and if they be a dying race, let us hope that in their last hours they will be able to recognize not simply the justice, but the generosity of the treatment which the white race, who are dispossessing them and entering into their heritage, are according them.[2]

As Deakin suggested, the states were left with the powers to deal with their own Aborigines. This meant that for a large part of the twentieth century, Aborigines experienced different forms of treatment, and lived under different policy frameworks, depending upon the state or territory in which they lived.

I noted earlier the gradual recuperation of the Aboriginal population in the early part of the twentieth century. Once it became apparent in the 1930s that Aborigines would not necessarily die out, and that there was a new "problem" in the growth of a so-called "half-caste" Aboriginal population, the solution was to make them biologically or culturally disappear. During the 1930s and early 1940s, some governments or the officials representing them, as in Western Australia and the Northern Territory, sought to breed Aborigines out through controlling marriage, especially between so-called "half-castes" and anybody else (Austin 1997; Haebich 1992). Those explicit breeding policies were soon phased out and overtaken by a regime of cultural assimilation, which dominated relations between non-Aboriginal and Aboriginal Australia up until the beginning of the 1970s. Under assimilation, Aborigines would give up their old ways and live in exactly the same way as everyone else. For some who adopted the ideology of cultural assimilation, the desire also seemed to be that the blackness of Aborigines, their outward marker of difference in the white nation, would gradually fade through intermarriage with whites.

The first phase of globalization, therefore, finally resolved itself, from about the 1930s, in deliberate efforts to hasten the demise of Aboriginal culture, collective identity, and group life through policies of assimilation. There were important exceptions such as Arnhem Land where traditional Aboriginal life was left largely intact until the discovery of minerals in the 1950s. Apart from missionary activity, attempts to modernize these Aborigines were minimal. But in many parts of Australia, the aim was that indigenous traditions, beliefs, and practices — entire forms of life — would disappear under government programs and policies aimed at educating Aborigines into the ways of modernity. This was "modernizing" Aborigines in order to better insert them, as individuals, into mainstream Australian life. Aboriginal culture and society, the argument went, was an anachronism, a relic of a past age that had no place in the present. Assimilation policies and programs, although inspired often enough by humanitarian impulses and leading to improvements in living conditions, certainly led to much sorrow and devastation (e.g., as a result of the theft of Aboriginal children from their parents), but they did not result in the disappearance of Aboriginal culture and traditions. On the contrary, there has been a resurgence of Aboriginal identity and culture in the latter part of the twentieth century.

The answer to the question of how Australia moved from that phase of triumphant western-centric globalization to the current situation of Aboriginal reassertion of culture, tradition, and claims, and at least partial recognition of these in the Australian polity, involves many parts. There is, for example, the more obviously global dimension. The situation of indigenous people in Australia today is part of a bigger story about indigenous people throughout the world, a story implicated in the *longues durée* of globalization. This includes transformations in the way that settlers, and westerners more generally, think about themselves, their societies and the other peoples of the world with whom they interact, and with whom they share certain elements of a common global fate.

The indigenous resurgence since about the 1960s is a worldwide phenomenon, at once intensely local and global in scope. Since the late 1960s, settler-nations have had to deal with articulate and politically astute indigenous peoples operating on the global stage (for a global anthology of indigenous voices, see Moody 1988a, b; see also Battiste 2000). It was in the 1960s that the "Red Power" movement emerged in the U.S. Initially spurred by the Civil Rights Movement, it sparked the revival of Native American identity and the resurgence of indigenous claims in national politics (Nagel 1997). The indigenous peoples of Canada experienced a similar process of revival, reacting against Trudeau's attempt in the late 1960s to legislate Native Status out of existence, and galvanized by objections to the development without consultation of national infrastructure across traditional indigenous lands (Niezen 2000; Webber 1994: 66–74). The Maori of New Zealand saw a revitalization of the Waitangi treaty process in the 1970s, and a rejuvenation of their culture (Joseph 2000). The claims of indigenous peoples of Latin America reemerged as a major political issue from the 1970s (Assies et al. 1999). Australia's indigenous peoples followed a similar pattern of resistance and rejuvenation.

Ronald Niezen argues that one of the distinguishing marks of the global indigenous movement is "the degree to which, unlike ethnonationalism, it is grounded in international networks." "Indigenous organizations defending local attachments to land and simple subsistence technologies," he points out, "make use of electronic media and technologies of communication and transportation to establish and maintain international connections" (2000: 120). Cohen and Rai (2000) argue that the global indigenous people's movement represents an excellent example of the way that the "local" and the "global" have become thoroughly intermeshed (Robertson 1995). "The heart of the paradox," they write, "is that the indigenous movements can only gain their support by asserting their difference, but they cannot succeed in the quest for recognition without showing their similarity to other oppressed peoples in other settings" (Cohen and Rai 2000: 10). The Working Definition of Indigenous Peoples adopted by the United Nations Working Group on Indigenous Populations reflects the sense of a generic indigenous people, the first part of the definition reading:

> Indigenous populations are composed of the existing descendants of peoples who inhabited the present territory of a country wholly or partially at the time when persons of a different culture or ethnic origin arrived there from other parts of the world, overcame them, and by conquest, settlement or other means, reduced them to a non-dominant or colonial situation; who today live more in conformity with their particular social, economic and cultural customs and traditions than with the institutions of the country of which they now form a part, under a state structure which incorporates mainly the national, social and cultural characteristics of other segments of the population which are predominant (reproduced in Wilmer 1993: 216).

Gaining recognition as indigenous peoples implies the development of a world society where claims cross national boundaries and move beyond national and regional governments to the domain of the international community, or the court of world opinion. From this angle, indigenous peoples defend their rights as a transnational grouping in need of specific forms of protection, in recognition of their peculiar circumstances as culturally different peoples trapped and marginalized within larger states. In articulating the need for various forms of protection of cultural rights, indigenous peoples have articulated a shared indigenous worldview that gains its particular expression in different locations. This worldview highlights, in general terms, the way that indigenous identity is thoroughly bound up with nature; that in fact, identity, nature, spirit, heritage, religion and so on are not separate spheres, but interwoven. As such, the indigenous worldview and identity are articulated as incommensurable with the worldviews and identities of western civilization and industrialization (Wilmer 1993).

The sources of indigenous power in the contemporary world, such as they exist, are typically spiritual and moral rather than military or economic. Indigenous peoples, together with their nonindigenous supporters including lawyers, historians, and other intellectuals, have used the political and legal traditions of the societies in which they operate, together with developing international law and human rights frameworks, to assert their claims and to embarrass governments. These efforts have been more or less successful, depending upon the political context and upon the moral sensibilities of those to whom they must appeal in their claims for recognition and justice (Maybury-Lewis 1997; Perry 1996; The Independent Commission on International Humanitarian Issues 1987). Indigenous peoples remain depressed and deprived communities within many first world countries, including Australia. However, in an age where "bountiful nature" seems increasingly threatened by depletion and global warming, they are now turned to as a source of deep knowledge about spiritual life, and living with nature, from at least some nonindigenous people. (This is especially true of Green movements.)

The new visibility of Australia's Aborigines and their specific claims has been part of a gradual process of transformation of the Australian nation-state and national identity since the Second World War. It has also been the result of the survival and rebuilding of Aboriginal communities during the twentieth century. The processes and developments have been local, regional, national, and global.

The events and aftermath of the Second World War, including the questioning and moral upheaval stemming from the Nuremberg trials, had a dramatic impact on racial thinking and politics across the world. Racial categories fell into disrepute with the revelations of Nazi atrocities. A series of United Nations sponsored studies and publications by eminent scientists from the late 1940s argued that race as a biological category was meaningless. Racial discrimination became a major international issue. This undermined the notions of race that stood behind the White Australia Policy, and further undermined already unstable claims about Aborigines' racial status that had influenced government and public perceptions about Aborigines' place in (or outside) Australian society. The war also led to economic and social advancement of the Aborigines drawn into the war economy and the defense forces. The experiences of Aborigines in and alongside the army in the Northern Territory, for example, and their interaction with whites as relative equals compared to their experience elsewhere, had a salutary effect for both whites and Aborigines (Rowley 1972: 332–340).

Important shifts in international relations, including the emergence of new international laws and treaties, and the phase of decolonization worldwide since 1947, made their contribution, especially in terms of the rise to consciousness of the plight of Australia's indigenous peoples, and the recognition of settler responsibility to deal with this ongoing situation. From the 1950s onward, there was international pressure on the Australian nation to improve settler/indigenous relations and to remove remaining forms of racial discrimination against Aborigines, like lower wages, unequal access to social security benefits, and lack of voting rights. Governments, fearing that Australia would be singled out as a pariah state like South Africa, felt and responded to this pressure, whether through policy initiatives or through public relations campaigns aimed at improving Australia's international reputation (Chesterman 2001a,b; Haebich 2000: chap. 7).

Since the 1960s, prominent Australian historians, political scientists, anthropologists, and other social commentators have highlighted the Aboriginal side of Australia's colonization, including the brutality with which Aborigines had often been treated. This revisionist history has not been without its critics, including Australia's current Prime Minister John Howard, who refers to it as "black-armband" history, a term invented by the historian Geoffrey Blainey. The brutality of the frontier period has recently been revisited in what has become known as "the history wars," stimulated by a controversial publication denying the extent of colonial massacres (Windschuttle 2002; for critique, see Macintyre and Clark [2003]; Manne [2003]). Nevertheless, since the 1960s consciousness of settler/indigenous relations has been fundamentally reshaped and made highly visible, after a long period of virtual invisibility.

The cultural debate and activities surrounding the 1988 Bicentenary placed Australia's initial act of dispossession in national focus. Indigenous protesters and their supporters marked this occasion, as they had previous days of national commemoration, with mourning ceremonies. The most well-known previous such occasion was the National Day of Mourning of 1938 organized by the Aboriginal activists William Ferguson, John Patten, and others to coincide with the 150th anniversary of the establishment of the New South Wales' colony (for an account, see Horner 1974).

The actions of Aborigines and their leaders have played a fundamental role in reshaping national consciousness of indigenous issues, and in advancing indigenous claims. Since the 1960s, and building on older indigenous actions and protests from the first half of the twentieth century, a series of Aboriginal protests has shaken the national complacency. Taking its lead from the American Civil Rights Movement, in 1965 a group of university students headed by the indigenous leader Charles Perkins staged the "Freedom Rides" through rural New South Wales, highlighting the everyday discrimination leveled at local indigenous people (for an account, see Curthoys 2002). Aboriginal activists and leaders took a leading role in the agitation leading up to the symbolically important 1967 Referendum (Bandler 1989). The resulting constitutional amendments — Aborigines would now be counted in the national census, and the federal government was allowed new powers to deal with Aboriginal affairs — were important, but the symbolic bringing in of Aborigines to the Australian nation was perhaps even more significant (Attwood et al. 1997).

The Wave Hill station walk-off staged by the Gurindji people in the Northern Territory from August 1966 brought to national attention the discriminatory wages and conditions experienced by Aboriginal people in the cattle industry, and the more disturbing question of Aboriginal land rights. The Gurindji made clear the broad nature of their demands in 1967 with a petition to the Governor General seeking land (which incorporated part of Wave Hill station) on the basis of "traditional rights" as well as the need for pastoral and mining enterprises for Aborigines (Coombs 1978: 158–160; Hardy 1978). These events have entered Australian folklore, and have been immortalized in a famous Australian song "From Little Things Big Things Grow" written by the non-indigenous singer Paul Kelly and the indigenous singer and activist Kev Carmody. Earlier, in 1963, after the Menzies government excised a large tract of land from the Arnhem Land Reserve for the mining of recently discovered bauxite on the Gove Peninsula, Yirrkala elders signed and presented to the Australian parliament their famous Bark Petition requesting that their rights to land be recognized (for a personal account of these events, see Yunupingu 1998; the text of the Bark Petition can be found in Reynolds 1989: 85–86).

As the call for land rights gained momentum, and Aborigines realized that a conservative government would not respond to their claims, Aboriginal activists created the Aboriginal Tent Embassy in Canberra in 1972, drawing international attention. This brilliant piece of political theater, assembling a tent and other structures on the grass outside Parliament House in the nation's capital, became a potent symbol for indigenous people of their outsider status within their own land. The Tent Embassy came and went during the 1970s, and has a presence to this day despite ongoing conflict with local authorities.

Since the early 1970s, the issue of land rights has remained on the political stage. Aboriginal land acts had been passed by the South Australian government in 1966 (*Aboriginal Land Trusts Act*) and the Victorian government in 1970 (*Aboriginal Lands Act*), although these did not provide inalienable rights to land (Bennett 1989: 29–30). In December 1976, the Liberal-National Fraser government passed the groundbreaking *Aboriginal Land Rights (Northern Territory) Act*, granting inalienable rights to land for traditional Aboriginal owners, and setting a trend other state governments followed with their own land rights acts.

Important national inquiries into Aboriginal deaths in custody (Commonwealth of Australia 1991) and into policies that resulted in stolen generations of Aboriginal children (Human Rights and Equal Opportunity Commission 1997) have been the source of national debate and hand-wringing, amid calls for political action including constitutional change, national apologies, compensation, and new policy initiatives. Australia-wide policies of taking Aboriginal children away from their families, for complex motives of assimilation and social welfare, devastating as these were for Aboriginal families and communities, have had the unintended effect of producing new forms of national Aboriginal unity, as indigenous groups began to meet at national forums to discuss commonality of experience, trauma and suffering and combined to lobby governments for reparations and policy changes (for accounts of these policies and their impact, see Human Rights and Equal Opportunity Commission 1997; Haebich 2000).

Two major legal decisions during the 1990s also transformed the way that many settler Australians viewed Aborigines and their claims. The historic High Court Mabo Decision of June 1992 (taking its name from one of the principal litigants in the case, the late Eddie Mabo from the island of Mer in the Torres Strait) dismissed the application of *terra nullius* to Australia and recognized, in legal terms, the survival of "native title" (traditional Aboriginal title to land) (*Mabo v. the State of Queensland*, No. 2, on June 3, 1992). The High Court ruled that native title could still exist in various parts of the country to the extent that various governments had not ruled specifically to dispossess the original Aboriginal owners (through the granting of land titles or through legislation). Significantly, and to the chagrin of some legal and political figures, this and later judgments on native title issues drew on legal precedents from other common law jurisdictions outside Australia. Some Australians welcomed the Mabo decision, but it was at the same time the subject of a hostile conservative campaign of opposition. The Keating Labor government passed a *Native Title Act*, which sought to reach a compromise between indigenous and nonindigenous interests and to compensate those Aborigines who had lost any hope of regaining traditional lands (Goot and Rowse 1994; for an account of the long struggle of the Mabo case, see Sharp 1996). It set up a Native Title Tribunal to administer the process. The Mabo ruling was elaborated by the High Court's Wik decision of December 1996 (*Wik Peoples v. State of Queensland*, 1996), which ruled that in certain circumstances native title could coexist with the pastoral leases that still existed in vast swathes of Australia. This legal situation demands complex negotiations between various indigenous and nonindigenous groups over the exact title to, and interest in, lands.

The Mabo and Wik decisions resulted in an ideological crisis for the settler nation state, and a long drawn out and continuing debate about the compromise needed to deal with the new legal situation. While there were calls for the state to extinguish native title all over Australia that, as one would expect, provoked considerable indigenous outrage and political resistance, other settler Australians called for acceptance and recognition of native title, seeing in the decision an opportunity to make some recompense for dispossession, and to move the settler nation into a truly postcolonial stage.

The course of the twentieth century has seen a gradual process of the political organization of Aborigines, from early autonomous groups protesting for rights and citizenship — Aboriginal Advancement and Progress committees, associations, fellowships, and leagues from the 1920s onwards — often at the subnational level, to more nationally organized movements like the Federal Council for the Advancement of Aboriginal and Torres Strait Islanders (FCAATSI). FCAATSI[3] emerged in the late 1950s as a major organization pursuing Aboriginal rights, and was the central political actor promoting the "Yes" vote in the 1967 Referendum (Bandler 1989). These organizations were frequently of mixed membership, and often non-Aborigines took leading and organizing roles. From the 1970s there emerged national Aboriginal organizations that were more strictly indigenous in membership and leadership, like the National Tribal Council, a successor to FCAATSI after a 1970 split over indigenous control of organizations and the pursuit of indigenous as opposed to simply equal rights (Read 1990; Attwood 2003). Organizations like the National Aboriginal Consultative Council (NACC) and the National Aboriginal Conference (NAC) in the 1970s and 1980s, and the current Aboriginal and Torres Strait Islander Commission (ATSIC) (1991–) and the Aboriginal Land Councils, were all formed and funded by national governments, in part to manage Aboriginal claims and aspirations in an orderly and efficient manner. Their legitimacy among indigenous peoples, although they have had members elected by popular Aboriginal vote, has been limited and often questioned. Nevertheless, they are forums for local, regional, and national Aboriginal voices. Other nongovernment-funded organizations like the Aboriginal Provisional Government (1990–) have been provocative, although limited in visibility and influence.

In understanding these developments throughout the latter half of the twentieth century, it becomes progressively difficult to distinguish between local, national, transnational, and global influences. The local had, indeed, been thoroughly brought together with the global, with events in far off places influencing and even transforming local attitudes, feelings, and political organization. Even before the advent of satellite communications and the internet, news of events elsewhere began filtering into indigenous communities across Australia, as one nonindigenous activist for Aboriginal rights pointed out in a magazine for Aborigines, *Smoke Signals*, in 1969:

> Now even the most illiterate and isolated Aborigine in this country is able to know what is going on in the world, and what he is missing … News bulletins inform him of progress elsewhere … and of the methods, achievements and policies of black men such as the Martin Luther Kings and Stokely Carmichaels of the world outside … Aborigines are no longer ignorant of their rights and opportunities as equals, and are no longer prepared to go on as if they were (cited in Attwood 2003: 315).

Factors influencing the explosion of indigenous consciousness in the late 1960s and early 1970s included not only the
transformed nature of Aboriginal life, with increased urban-
ization, better education, and the gradual movement off the
missions, stations, and reserves, but also major developments
elsewhere, like decolonization movements in Africa, and the
Red Power Movement, the American Indian Movement, the
Civil Rights Movement, black consciousness (Moody 1988b:
294–295), and even the Black Power movement in the U.S. —
the latter had a brief flowering among indigenous activists in
the early 1970s, mainly in and around Sydney.

Indigenous peoples, in Australia and elsewhere, have
engaged with globalizing processes in order to assert their
"traditional" claims. The effective resistance of indigenous
peoples since the latter half of the twentieth century has been
a story of transnational collaboration. Transnational and global
organizations now represent indigenous peoples around the
world. These provide forums for comparison of situation and
status of indigenous peoples in different countries, and for the
development of political strategies, both intra- and internationally. The World Council of Indigenous Peoples (WCIP) was
formed after a world conference held in Port Alberni, British
Columbia in 1975. Indigenous people from Australia attended
the first meetings leading to the formation of the WCIP and
have been actively involved since, including hosting the Third
General Assembly in Canberra in 1981. These and other international forums, including most importantly the United
Nations Working Group on Indigenous Populations, like earlier imperial forums, have provided avenues for the investiga-
tion and pursuit of indigenous claims (Sanders 1980; Wilmer
1993).

Since the 1970s, Australian Aboriginal leaders, activists, and writers have traveled the world, participating in conferences and forums. They watch international developments closely, at the same time playing an active role in shaping those developments. (One example would be the articulation of an international discourse on indigenous rights, expressed in documents such as the "Draft Declaration of the Rights of Indigenous Populations".) Despite continuing and powerful forms of exclusion, Aborigines play an active role in Australian cultural, artistic, sporting, and political life. The indigenous art movement, with its dot and bark paintings, has become a significant international export and source of international interest in Australia. Aboriginal culture is promoted heavily as one of the major tourist attractions of Australia.

There is a certain irony, perhaps, in the fact that where an earlier phase of globalization involved processes through which Aborigines were virtually destroyed in Australia, Australia's indigenous peoples have grasped the horns of contemporary globalization in order to creatively resist, and even reverse, that ongoing devastation. The strategy, however, is ambiguous, precarious, and unpredictable. Although the international dimension of indigenous politics is clearly important, one should not overstate the strength of the indigenous position in terms of international law and developing norms. It remains the case in Australia that the nation-state and its institutions are the most important avenues through which Aborigines must achieve their aims. They must engage with and cultivate the national community and national and state governments. Thus, while the Howard government received strong international criticism from 1998 onward after it introduced controversial amendments to the *Native Title Act* in response to the Wik decision, this did not stop the legislation from passing through the parliaments and it remains in place to this day. International pressure included the embarrassment of being called before the United Nations to defend the amendments, which the UN's Committee on the Elimination of Racial Discrimination later deemed to be discriminatory (United Nations Office of the High Commissioner for Human Rights 1999).

Similarly, the more significant aims of Aborigines can only be achieved in Australia by cultivating national sentiment in such a way that non-Aboriginal Australians feel that things ought to be done to benefit Aborigines. This is reflected in many indigenous political demands, and in the tenor in which they are made, including appeals by some indigenous leaders for justice in order to "heal" the whole Australian nation, within which they include themselves as equal yet distinctive members (see, e.g., Dodson 1999). As in other contexts, although the claims of Australia's indigenous peoples pose challenges for the settler-nation, the explicit demands are not necessarily, or even typically, for complete separation and the creation of an indigenous state or states, but for forms of autonomy, self-government, and land rights within the already existing Australian nation-state, and for forms of symbolic and economic redress for past and ongoing injustice.

While indigenous peoples have made use of intensified globalization to further their political aims, globalization also presents them with threats to their ongoing existence, to their forms of life, identities, and to the things that they hold most dear.

The calls from "globalists" for the opening up and liberalization of economies and places, creating the one global market place, fly in the face of indigenous claims for control over the lands, and the culture, that remain to them. This has been felt most potently by indigenous Australians in debates over infrastructure development, mining, agriculture, logging, and fishing, where these clash with Aboriginal land rights and native title. Indigenous claims over such lands, waters, and sacred places involve forms of restriction and closure, and frequently represent "impediments" to development in the eyes of those who wish to exploit Australia's resources.

Some multicultural discourses are also potentially at odds with indigenous claims and aspirations, even if proponents of multiculturalism would be appalled to think so. For example, in support of expanding Australia's population through high levels of immigration some theorists of multiculturalism have argued that Australia has a moral duty to the world to share the burden of global (not simply refugee) population (see, e.g., Cope and Kalantzis 2000). They argue that population problems need to be settled globally, and that Australia, with a large and vacant land mass at its disposal, has no right to keep this to itself. These advocates remain silent on the relationship between their arguments for population expansion and notions of native title and indigenous control over resources. Such global discourse updates and rejuvenates the old settler argument that Australia was an empty space to be filled by British peoples, by claiming that it is now to be filled by the diverse peoples of the world.

Notions of global sharing, of creolization, hybridity and cultural borrowing, imply that all cultures are ripe for the picking. Such notions, however, have a particularly negative resonance with Australia's Aborigines. Often, global cultural sharing is experienced by them as cultural theft and threat. In fact, the political trend among Australia's Aborigines has been in the opposite direction, calling for better methods of defending and protecting indigenous culture and heritage from exploitation. They have fought for greater forms of legislative protection, engaging with intellectual and cultural property, copyright, and heritage laws. From the perspective of many Aborigines, they should have the right to decide how and under what circumstances their languages, art forms, myths, and sacred and other knowledge are accessed and presented to the outside world. From this perspective, the Internet and other forms of mass reproduction present a threat to identity, and the possibility of deeper forms of penetration and exploitation of indigenous cultures in Australia (Janke 1998).

The use and proliferation of the Internet and other forms of communication, Havemann (2000) argues, also pose a threat to traditional indigenous culture and to local indigenous communities by exposing them to global influences and undermining traditional authority structures. On the other hand, new forms of communication and transport have opened up new possibilities for indigenous peoples to gain recognition throughout the world for their cultural achievements (Smith and Ward 2000), and thus to build a moral community willing to acknowledge their case for protection. In Australia, as in Canada, indigenous people's movements have a major network of websites at their disposal (Havemann 2000: 29). Given the take-up of these new communication resources, the "network" aspect of contemporary indigenous politics in Australia is particularly important. These developments have also given rise to new economic possibilities, including the economic benefits obtained from interest in indigenous productions (art, music, and other forms). They have presented new ways for indigenous peoples to remain and sustain themselves in remote traditional places, carrying on with traditional practices, as the result, for example, of the global interest in eco-tourism. Indigenous ownership of and control over international tourist destinations such as Uluru and its surrounding areas, and Kakadu National Park, which is on the World Heritage listing, provides desperately needed income, resources, and employment opportunities for local traditional landowners.

The cultural resurgence of indigenous peoples in Australia (as elsewhere) involves a corrective to the idea that cultural globalization involves the necessary homogenization of culture or even the emergence of a common world culture. While mass culture influences, from baseball caps and T-shirts to other signs of transnational commodification, can be seen in indigenous communities even in remote areas of Australia, such cultural trappings do not simply replace other forms of indigenous culture or identity.

This also complicates the notion of detraditionalization, for, despite intensive government and missionary attempts in the past to smash indigenous culture and the authority of elders, indigenous people today assert the strength of, and their belief in, their indigenous traditions and authority structures, even as they engage in nontraditional modern Australian practices. Here is a case of modernity and tradition — or indigenous worldviews — meeting, clashing, compromising, eyeing each other off, and invading each other.

Examples include the hybrid forms of Christianity relevant for many indigenous peoples in the past and today, where more "modern" Christian beliefs exist alongside more traditional belief systems and "dreaming" stories. As Edwards points out, sometimes this means that two belief systems exist alongside each other within the one person or community:

> Aboriginal Christians in churches where traditional belief systems are still strong have tended to compartmentalize these systems with the Christian stories. They have been willing to accept the validity of dreaming stories at the same time as acknowledging God as creator. Dreaming stories do not assume the logic of Western thought and they see no incongruity in affirming both belief systems (1994: 81).

John Harris has described the situation of Aboriginal Christianity in Central Australia:

> Perhaps the most striking use of Aboriginal cultural expression in the Christian context has been associated with the Baptist missions in central Australia among the Walpiri, Gurindji and Alyawarra people. At places like Lajamanu, Yuendumu and Kalkaringi, a vibrant, distinctively Aboriginal Christian church is emerging, typified by Christian *purlapas* (corroborees), Christian iconographs and indigenous music, noticeably the use of the old "law song" as a medium for credal statements (1990: 863).

Aboriginal traditions are not simply rooted in the past and unchangeable, despite the attempts of colonialist texts to characterize them in this way. Indigenous traditions, as indigenous spokespersons have pointed out, have the capacity to change and adapt to new conditions. Like western culture itself, indigenous cultures have been transformed by the reception and acceptance of discourses of human rights. Some traditional practices are no longer acceptable to contemporary Aborigines in the context of these human rights frameworks, while other traditional beliefs and practices remain intact or have been transformed. Even before the arrival of Europeans, Aboriginal culture and tradition developed and adapted over 40,000 or 60,000 years, albeit at a slower pace than has been evident since 1788 (Edwards 1994; Stanner 1979). Where traditions and cultures have been deemed lost or destroyed, individuals and groups are actively reclaiming them via the Internet and by access to old records and writings, including those of anthropologists and ethnographers. Aboriginal people living in cities return, sometimes physically, sometimes imaginatively, to the places where their identities are embedded and from which they continue to draw strength.

This very situation has given rise to important political battles in Australia, especially around legal and political struggles for land rights or native title and the protection of sites of spiritual significance. Courts have tended to operate with more rigid ideas about identity, tradition, and cultural continuity than have many indigenous peoples, as the Yorta Yorta of Victoria and New South Wales were unfortunate enough to discover in their recent failed Native Title case.

The Yorta Yorta had, since time immemorial, occupied an area of about 20,000 km^2 on both sides of what is now the border between New South Wales and Victoria. The lands and waters, including part of Australia's largest river, the Murray, had been the source of their livelihood and of their spiritual life and identity. They first experienced the full assault of colonization in the late 1830s when cattle and sheep runs were taken up in their lands. They were gradually dispossessed of their lands from this time. In the succeeding years, some of them were dispersed to other areas of Victoria and New South Wales, to missions, stations, and reserves. In a bitter irony, this very dispersal formed part of the case against them, since it was claimed that traditional connection with land, once it had been physically severed, could not be reinstated. Yorta Yorta people disputed this argument, claiming that physical separation from lands had not meant irrevocable spiritual separation, and that for many Yorta Yorta descendants of today the connection with traditional lands remains vital to their identity. Not only that, but these descendants had responsibilities and duties in relation to the lands and waters that had to be met and fulfilled (some of this testimony can be found in a recent work by the Yorta Yorta elder Wayne Atkinson [2001]).

The Yorta Yorta Native Title ruling was immensely significant because it was seen as the most important test case for native title in the more closely settled parts of Australia. Unlike Aborigines in places like Arnhem Land and other parts of the Northern Territory, who had been relatively untouched by colonization until the twentieth century, the Yorta Yorta had been in close and continuing contact with settlers since the late 1830s. Their traditional lands were now like a patchwork, with many important interests competing for resources and unfettered access. The Yorta Yorta could only claim parcels of unalienated Crown land nestled into freehold areas, towns, parks, and so on (Atkinson 2001; Dodson 1995).

After battling their way through a mediation process under the auspices of the Native Title Tribunal, and two adverse Federal Court cases where their claim was pitted against a formidable array of legal experts, business interests and State governments, the High Court upheld the earlier decision that "the tide of history" had swept away their native title claim. Among the many arguments involved in the case, it was accepted by the courts that the Yorta Yorta no longer lived in their traditional ways or abided by their traditional beliefs and rites. In coming to this conclusion, the first judge to find against the Yorta Yorta, Justice Olney, measured current beliefs and practices against the recorded reminiscences of the settler and amateur ethnographer Edward Curr (1883), who had himself participated in their dispossession. Justice Olney dismissed the significance of the oral testimony from Yorta Yorta elders and younger members taken during the Court's proceedings, about ongoing adherence to traditional beliefs and practices (*The Members of the Yorta Yorta Aboriginal Community v. The State of Victoria & Ors* [1998] 1606 FCA [18 December 1998]).

Despite these adverse rulings, the Yorta Yorta remain defiant. Although deeply hurt by the implication that they no longer existed as a people, they continue their struggle for recognition, and to rebuild their community in their traditional area. At present, they are considering taking their case into the international arena, pursuing their claim through the United Nations.

The discourse of land rights and the indigenous resurgence more generally have opened up new complexities for nonindigenous Australians. Where once settler Australians imagined that they formed one homogeneous nation occupying the entire continent, in more recent times they have had to contemplate the idea that different peoples occupy the same continent. While nonindigenous and indigenous Australians have commonalities and shared experiences, they also have significant differences. These differences are not easily accommodated within older liberal notions of what a nation is. It is difficult for many settler Australians to reconcile the value of "equality", for example, with various forms of special rights — to land, to culture — that indigenous people continue to demand. National space has become more internally complex with the acceptance of land rights and sacred sites.

For some nonindigenous Australians, such forms of recognition deeply challenge their sense of national belonging. The assertion by Aborigines that the land has meanings that only the indigenous groups of particular locales can understand is a challenge to the nationalist understanding of the exclusive relationship between nation and land. While this has fundamental economic dimensions — for example those indigenous meanings can clash with the desires of miners, farmers, pastoralists, or tourists — it also has a symbolic dimension. It cannot help but unsettle settlers, returning them to issues of land settlement they believed had been resolved in the past.

The clash between settler nationalist assertions and indigenous aspirations can be illustrated by reactions to the handing back of Ayers Rock — now renamed Uluru — to traditional owners by the Hawke government in 1985. The main argument against the handing back was a nationalist one: that Ayers Rock was a central symbol for all Australians. A national survey at the time showed that non-Aboriginal Australians were upset at the handing over of a "national symbol" to one small group of Aborigines (Australian National Opinion Polls 1985). Conservative federal opposition parliamentarians argued vigorously against the hand-over. One argued that the Rock as a geological formation was actually more significant to non-Aboriginal Australians than to the traditional owners, a "part of our psyche, because Australians feel deeply about it and love it."[4] Another referred to "the horror which swept this country when the ... government took this national symbol away from 99.99 percent of Australians." In a long speech, he elaborated upon the reasons for this purported horror, referring to the deep emotional attachment that most Australians felt for the Rock. "It stirs deep feelings in all of us. A visit to Ayers Rock has become something that every Australian aspires to do. It has almost become a pilgrimage for some," he argued. He claimed that Australians had "become strangers in their own country" and that most were outraged about the decision. Another parliamentarian argued that Australians were watching angrily as the government gave away a key national symbol — "the best known and best loved symbol of our Australian heritage." He saw the handing back as an accusation of cultural impoverishment of non-Aboriginal Australia. All of the natural wonders were culturally significant to non-Aborigines, just as they were for Aborigines. He raised the spectre of Australians becoming "tourists in their own land."[5] Yet another pointed to massive community opposition and shock at the transfer of "Australia's best known natural monument to an ethnic group [sic] with very limited proven rights to such an area... ." He argued that Ayers Rock was "a piece of every Australian's backyard" and that its hand-over would mean not only the partitioning of Australia, but would put "a mental partition in the minds of most Australians." He warned that this would lead to racial strife as Aborigines were perceived as thieves of the national inheritance. "No longer will the Aboriginal be seen just as socially different," he claimed, "he will now be seen universally as having taken something that belongs to all Australians."[6] It was clear that for some people deep feelings were aroused. A letter, published in *The Australian* newspaper in March 1985, claimed that the decision would "allow people to physically possess the spiritual heart of this nation," and was "a knife thrust that wounds every Australian."[7]

Since it was handed back to traditional owners, the site has been under joint Aboriginal and public management. It is well known that traditional owners do not want tourists to climb the rock, but they do not have the power to prevent such activities. Recently there was renewed controversy when tribal elders representing the traditional owners decided to close the site for a period of time as part of a mourning process. Tourist companies complained of losses, and others argued that Australia simply could not afford to close such an important national icon if it was to continue to gain from international tourism.

Since the 1980s, there have been other major controversies surrounding the interaction between Aboriginal meanings, beliefs, and relationships with land and broader national and other interests. In 1991 Prime Minister Bob Hawke was subjected to ridicule by some non-Aboriginal Australians, including then Liberal Opposition leader John Hewson, when he vetoed mining at Coronation Hill in the Northern Territory's Kakadu National Park. Against intense and bitter opposition from members of his own Cabinet, Hawke accepted the concerns of the Jawoyn, the indigenous owners of the land, that mining would release the serpent god Bula from the ground, wreaking untold havoc and damage. In defending his decision, Hawke explicitly placed Jawoyn beliefs on the same level with spiritual beliefs endorsed by mainstream Christianity (Hawke 1994: 505–510; Gelder and Jacobs 1998: chap. 4). From the mid-1990s, there was a long drawn out national controversy known as the "Hindmarsh Island Affair," where a group of local Aboriginal women sought to prevent the building of a bridge between the mainland and Hindmarsh Island in South Australia by claiming that the area was sacred to women. The bridge was later allowed to go ahead after a Royal Commission and a High Court ruling (Simons 2003). These events reveal underlying and unresolved tensions about the relationship between indigenous people's rights and the broader interests of the nation.

On the other hand, there has been a significant acceptance at the political level that indigenous peoples have specific interests that need to be protected by forms of legislation and by other special measures not available to nonindigenous Australians. In Australia's Northern Territory there has been some recognition by the courts of the ongoing validity of traditional Aboriginal law and forms of punishment and rectification in certain circumstances. (This has, nevertheless, been a controversial development, much criticized by some nonindigenous commentators.)

There is evidence also of broader levels of adjustment on the part of the nonindigenous population, indicated by the commitment to a reconciliation process since the early 1990s. The official reconciliation movement was launched by the Hawke and Keating governments with the setting up of the Council for Aboriginal Reconciliation in 1991. The Council, made up of indigenous and nonindigenous members, worked for its ten years of legislated existence to build trust between indigenous and nonindigenous communities across Australia. It worked to educate nonindigenous Australians about the history of settler/indigenous relations, about living indigenous cultures and communities, and about indigenous needs and claims. It promoted notions of living together and sharing, while accommodating important differences and accepting the need for respect for indigenous culture, traditions, and relationships with land and waters (see documents, reports etc. in Reconciliation and Social Justice Library 2003). In its wake came a grassroots reconciliation movement with branches all over Australia. Local councils, schools, churches, small groups of like-minded citizens, and larger organizations like Australians for Native Title and Reconciliation (ANTaR) formed reconciliation committees and groups and staged small- and large-scale events throughout the 1990s. In 2000, hundreds of thousands of nonindigenous and indigenous Australians walked in Reconciliation marches in Australia's major cities and in its regional and rural towns.

This reconciliation process, and the people's movement that it spawned, revealed another side to Australian nationalism, which had been gathering momentum since the 1960s. This more inclusive, "indigenizing" settler nationalism develops and elaborates an impulse that has existed for a long time in Australian settler nationalism, fore-grounding the importance of the Aboriginal contribution to national culture. It is characterized by an attitude of mourning and sorrow in relation to past and contemporary forms of oppression of Australia's Aborigines. It involves an honoring of, and a desire to make reparation to, Aborigines, which was absent in earlier dominant forms of Australian settler nationalism (e.g., white Australia nationalism), and views the actions of the settler nation in the past with a more critical eye. It adopts a position that calls upon the nation to reconstruct itself through a fuller recognition of Aborigines and their claims as a central component of the national identity. These impulses are evident in a range of phenomena including artistic and literary works, histories and other social commentaries (e.g., see Graham

1994; Brennan 1995; Tacey 1995; Read 2000), the discourse of politicians, the reconciliation movement and related events such as "National Sorry Day" and the "Sea of Hands," and organizations such as the Journey of Healing Committee. This form of settler nationalism responded to the pressure and calls for civil rights, equality and specific indigenous rights to land and cultural expression from the 1960s, by arguing that such forms of recognition were a way of including Aborigines more fully within the Australian nation; in the process, Australia's national identity would be transformed in a positive way.

Indigenizing settler nationalism represents an important emotional shift for settler Australians. It involves a reaching out to embrace Aborigines as full moral members of a shared Australian nation. The claim is that through such an act the Australian nation would become less a settler nation than a postcolonial "tapestry" nation with Aborigines accorded a central, identity-giving place. Their cultural heritage, their long and deep spiritual connection with Australian lands, given as a "gift" to the national community, would indigenize the Australian nation as a whole.

This recognition of the importance of the spiritual connection of Aborigines with land at the same time allows settler Australians to feel secure in their own national identity, and in their connection with place. By sharing culture and heritage, under the tutelage of an expanded and transformed vision of national identity, it is claimed that all the different peoples of Australia will feel a sense of belonging to a common land and to a shared, diverse, and yet civil, public space. There are elements of appropriation of Aboriginality sometimes involved in this (see Moran 1998), but there is also an ethic of sharing that does not need to involve the disappearance of important differences between indigenous and nonindigenous relationships with land. In its best guise, it involves a "strange multiplicity" (Tully 1995): the land is traversed by different meanings that converse rather than conflict with each other (Read 2000) — a dream perhaps, but not such a bad one for a globalizing world.

Two council workers, John and Eddie, are sipping coffee and telling me of their feelings about and interactions with the local Iraqis, refugees who have recently arrived in their town and disturbed the normal patterns of life. Most of the talk is pretty negative. The Iraqis, they say, have little respect for Australians or, for that matter, for their own women or for animals. They only want the very best for themselves. They are ungrateful. When Iraqis realized that the furniture given to them by local charities was secondhand, they put it out in the street. Somehow, some of them had purchased expensive cars after being here only a few months. They had little interest in anyone apart from other Iraqis. They would walk by and simply ignore you, as if you didn't exist, as if it wasn't your hometown that they had come to live in.

Interrupting each other, or speaking in turns, John and Eddie tell the story of the closing down by health inspectors of an Iraqi butcher when it was discovered that the animals were being slaughtered in the backyard. Before it was closed, locals who went in there and tried to buy sausages were responded to with a shrug. There only seemed to be large chunks of meat hanging on hooks. Not so long ago, it was a "normal" Aussie butcher.

Waving his arm over toward the mosque that had been on the outskirts of town for more than 40 years, John told how those who ran it, Albanian families who had lived in the area for generations, had first invited the Iraqis in to worship but did not want them back anymore because of the mess they left behind, and because of the way that they treated the place and other worshippers.

More disturbingly, there was an Iraqi house that was raided by ASIO (Australian Security Intelligence Organisation) some months earlier, but it was kept quiet, and did not even make the papers. They had heard about it from a friend who lived nearby and who had watched the raid in broad daylight. At this house, according to John and Eddie, they found sacks of superphosphate. Why would someone who was not a farmer have so much of it? The answer was self-evident: it was there to make bombs. John had no doubt that there were terrorist "sleepers" hiding among the Iraqi families. The sooner we got them all back to Iraq, the better.

Once Eddie leaves, and just before I turn the tape recorder on to begin our interview, John says in a quieter, far less combative tone: "I'm really not a racist you know." That's not what all this was about. This problem with the Iraqis was something different. In the course of the interview, John went on to explain how the Iraqis were, unlike the Italians and Greeks and other Europeans who make up multicultural Australia, "centuries behind us," and he had extreme doubts about their capacity to ever "assimilate" into the Australian way of life.

Globalization, it is frequently asserted, involves the stretching of political community beyond the nation-state, and allows for a range of overlapping and intermeshing forms of citizenship (including rights and duties) from the local to the national, regional, and global. There is no doubt that, at least to some extent, this has occurred, and has transformed the way that many of us live. Apart from the need arising from global economic interrelatedness, the sense of belonging to a single globe and to global humanity has contributed to the emergence of forms of global governance (see the description of the cosmopolitan project in Held et al. 1999: 449–450; see also Held 1995). International human rights laws, agreements and protocols, a global response to humanitarian crises and to the plight of refugees, transnational nongovernmental organizations (NGOs) that act as important political players in world affairs: all of these things have been transformative.

On the other hand, and as the above recounting of my interaction with John and Eddie suggests, there are important senses in which the Australian political community has not been stretched to incorporate certain kinds of people. A national community is a form of ethical or moral community. While liberal nationalism can entail forms of internationalism that call upon nations to extend their provisions to some extent beyond the boundaries of the national community, this is typically limited and the primary ethical and social responsibility is felt for conationals (Miller 1993, 1995; Cole 2000). In the case of asylum seekers, the nation, this important form of social closure, has interacted with intensified globalization in ways related to underlying anxieties about exposure to an unruly world.

The asylum seeker, the "illegal immigrant," is a potent symbol of the permeability of boundaries, and because of this has come to represent an amorphous threat to national sovereignty. When people speak of asylum seekers with any sense of alarm or concern, rational assessment frequently goes out the window: the language quickly turns to images of engulfment or flood, and to worst-case scenarios. Terrorism, especially after September 11, adds one more important layer to these threat perceptions.

Australia has a history of receiving refugees, based on a complex and shifting mix of humanitarian impulses, a sense of international responsibility, relations with other countries, and the perceived needs of the nation-state (Rivett 2001). After the Second World War, when Britain could not supply sufficient numbers of immigrants, eastern and central European refugees were a major source of population and labor, feeding Australian postwar reconstruction and economic and industrial development. In 1947, Australia signed an agreement with the International Refugee Organization to receive a minimum of 12,000 per year of Europe's estimated 40 million displaced persons. When the scheme ended in 1953 to 1954, Australia had resettled more than 170,000 refugees (United Nations High Commissioner for Refugees 2000: 13; Jordens 2001). The United Nations High Commissioner for Refugees (UNHCR) reports that in the 25 years after 1945 Australia had accepted 350,000 refugees, mainly from Europe. After the dismantling of the White Australia Policy in 1973, Australia accepted more than 185,000 refugees from Indochina, the largest number after the United States and Canada (United Nations High Commissioner for Refugees 2000: 181–182).

In its current immigration program (85,000 to 110,000 per year), Australia accepts about 4000 offshore refugees each year as part of its perceived international obligations as a signatory to the UN's 1951 Convention and 1967 Protocol. This is made up of those who have been processed by the UNHCR in other countries and have been awaiting resettlement elsewhere. Each year, Australia also accepts about 4000 people who arrive legally (i.e., with various types of visas) and who then apply for refugee status, and unauthorized arrivals who claim asylum. Others who do not fit the strict criteria of refugees may be accepted in Australia under other aspects of the Humanitarian Program — the Special Humanitarian and Special Assistance categories — bringing the annual numbers up to around 12,000 (Crock and Saul 2002: 12; McMaster 2001: 63).

Most refugees are now a surplus to Australia's needs. No longer in search of a bulky labor supply — fodder for factories, public works, and other menial labor — Australian governments are now far more selective, preferring immigrants with high levels of capital and skill, and who will most easily adapt to Australian society and its modernized economy. This situation is of course characteristic of other places, with many privileged countries that previously accepted refugees and semiskilled workers from poorer countries now closing this avenue for movement (Castles 2002). Globalization, as Bauman (1998) points out, means high mobility for the most privileged, and low mobility for those in desperate need.

Until the 1970s when Indochinese boat people began arriving on Australia's northern coast, Australia had almost no experience with large-scale unauthorized immigration. Australia's geographical isolation and lack of land borders meant that it had for a long time been an unlikely destination for such entry. However, improvements in transport and communications, and the explosive growth of refugees and displaced persons as a result of wars and persecution (more than 22 million "persons of concern" worldwide, according to UNHCR [United Nations High Commissioner for Refugees 2000: 10]), have meant that people in places far from Australia, and globally organized people-smuggling rackets, have now come to view Australia as a possible destination. Asylum seekers from the Middle East and

Asia are, for example, now flown to Malaysia, Singapore, or Indonesia and, with the aid of smugglers and corrupt local officials, attempt to find their way by boat to the Australian continent or its coastal islands.

Australian governments have become increasingly hostile to those who enter Australia in ways that it deems illegal, especially by boat. This was exemplified by the well-known events of 2001 to 2002, when the Australian Navy, under government instruction, began to stop boats of asylum seekers from entering Australian territory, either towing them back to international waters, or taking them by force to places outside Australian territory for processing. The first and most famous of these actions involved a Norwegian ship.

On Sunday, August 26, 2001, a Norwegian sea captain, Arne Rinnan of the container vessel *MV Tampa*, responded to a call from the Rescue Co-Ordination Centre Australia to pick up 80 or so passengers from a stricken vessel. The sinking ship, which turned out to be the Indonesian ferry *Palapa* carrying 438 rather than 80 people, was stranded between the coasts of Indonesia and Australia. Following maritime convention and Norwegian seafaring traditions, Captain Rinnan took the passengers on board and provided them with food and shelter. Of the 438, 433 were asylum seekers. Initially headed toward Indonesia's Sunda Strait, he was persuaded by protesting asylum seekers to steer for Christmas Island, an Australian territory far off Australia's northwestern coast and close to Indonesia. The asylum seekers, he explained in an interview with the BBC, threatened to injure themselves, even to throw themselves overboard, should he attempt to take them back to Indonesia. They told him they only wanted to go to Australia. To Rinnan's astonishment and dismay, once he had decided to sail for Christmas Island he was informed by an official from the Department of Immigration and Multicultural Affairs that he would not be allowed to land on Australian territory (BBC News 2001a). For its part, the Indonesian government, angered by what its Foreign Minister Hassan Wirajuda called Australia's "megaphone diplomacy" (quoted in Mares 2002: 124), refused the landing of the *MV Tampa* on Indonesian soil, its armed forces threatening military action if it attempted to do so (BBC News 2001b). Moored in international waters off Christmas Island, the asylum seekers sat on the deck in the evening looking calmly at the coast, and would remain calm, Captain Rinnan told the BBC, only as long as they could see the island. He, his crew, and the asylum seekers waited in the heat (BBC News 2001a).

The days that followed saw a charged standoff between the Australian, Norwegian, and Indonesian governments. Some of the asylum seekers went on hunger strike. On Wednesday, August 29, and precipitated by the *MV Tampa*'s entry into Australian territorial waters — Rinnan tired of the failure of the Australian authorities to provide promised medical and other assistance, and he believed that the delay was putting lives in danger — members of Australia's elite special forces (the SAS) boarded the *MV Tampa* and took control. Eight days after they were picked up by the *MV Tampa*, the asylum seekers were transferred to an Australian navy vessel, the *HMAS Manoora*, and were dispersed, via Papua New Guinea, for UNHCR processing to the tiny island of Nauru, and to New Zealand. This new government strategy for dealing with boat people, involving agreements between the Australian and other governments in the region, was dubbed the "Pacific Solution." Many of the *MV Tampa*'s asylum seekers, it was discovered, were Afghans fleeing the ruthless Taliban regime (for detailed accounts of these events, see MacCallum 2002; Mares 2002; Marr and Wilkinson 2003).

An expensive military action to guard Australia's vast coastline was then imposed by the Australian government in order to turn away any future refugee ships.[1] (The militarization of border protection in relation to asylum seekers is an issue that I will return to.) The ships that came, like the *MV Tampa*, were either turned back, or disposed of via the "Pacific Solution" to Nauru and Papua New Guinea's Manus Island. Marr and Wilkinson in their book *Dark Victory* (2003) provide a detailed account of the extraordinary behind-the-scenes maneuverings between government and its agencies as the new policy was put into effect. They also provide a powerful account of what transpired off Australian shores, tales of sinking boats full of desperate asylum seekers being towed back out to sea, or followed by naval boats until the very last moment before their passengers were saved. They write of the confusion and demoralization of Australian military personnel called upon to act against their better judgment and instincts (see also accounts in Mares 2002). The new strategy, although expensive and internationally embarrassing, was very successful: in the period between January and August 2002, not a single unauthorized asylum seeker arrived in Australia by boat.[2]

The *MV Tampa* incident, which attracted international attention including angry criticism from countries within the region and from Scandinavia, was situated within both domestic and global contexts. With its policy of "mandatory detention of all persons without authority to be in Australia," introduced by a Labor government in the early 1990s and adhered to by succeeding governments, Australia already had a global reputation as one of the toughest countries in its dealing with "unautho-rised" asylum seekers (see Human Rights Watch and Amnesty International reports from the 1990s onward). Nevertheless, concerned by the increase of boat people entering Australia from its largely unguarded northern and western coasts in the late 1990s — from 921 in 1998 to 1999 to 4175 in 1999 to 2000 and 4137 in 2000 to 2001[3] — the Howard government decided to send a message to the rest of the world that Australia was "no soft touch" for people smugglers and their quarry of "illegal immigrants." Apart from its devastating consequences for the ship's crew and for the asylum seekers, the government response on the *MV Tampa* was a political theater of a spectacular variety.

The *MV Tampa* incident and its aftermath also reflects the relationship between long political traditions and the forces of globalization. Australia has always had a tightly controlled immigration program: the notion of refugees self-selecting themselves, as it were, was viewed with greater abhorrence by Australians because of that tradition of tight bureaucratic regulation. When Australia took in thousands of Europe's dis-placed persons after the Second World War as part of its efforts to "populate or perish," it was immigration officers who scoured the camps in search of the very best stock who would fit in most easily in "white Australia." This sort of approach — searching for the best stock — still stands behind Australia's preferred way of dealing with refugees, even if the emphasis upon "whiteness" has disappeared. This was exemplified by Prime Minister John Howard's 2001 elec-tion campaign slogan "We will decide who comes into this country and the circumstances in which they come here." It was also exemplified by the tough stance and approach of the Labor Opposition.

Although the Howard government claimed that its actions in response to the *MV Tampa* crisis were inspired by increases in the numbers of unauthorized arrivals (see Ministerial Statements 2001), the numbers were still small by world standards. It is well known that two-thirds of claims for asylum in the world are made in European Union countries (Jupp 2003). Asylum seekers, and immigration more generally, have become large political issues in a number of those countries, with swelling support for conservative and populist parties with anti-immigration messages. Only a small percentage of such claims for asylum are made in Australia (Crock and Saul 2002: xvi). The burden of dealing with the world's refugees, internally displaced persons, and other people of concern is overwhelmingly borne by the poorer and underdeveloped countries of Africa and Asia (United Nations High Commissioner for Refugees 2000; Castles 2002: 174). From this perspective, the Australian reaction to asylum seekers since the 1990s, and even more so after the *MV Tampa* crisis, seems wildly out of proportion to the real threat, and to the possible drain on public resources. How is one then to understand this phenomenon?

Cast in its best light, such actions could be seen as a rational and moral response to a world problem: that is the import of government "humanitarian" rationale for the policies. By enacting "zero tolerance," the Australian government claimed to be attacking the repugnant activity of people smuggling, potentially saving the lives of would-be boat people who would be deterred from seeking out the services of people smugglers and, furthermore, protecting the rights of those "legitimate" and bona fide refugees who were patiently awaiting their turn for resettlement. It could be argued that the controversial policy of mandatory detention of unauthorized arrivals responds to issues of legality and control that any government must address where asylum seekers are concerned. It seems eminently sensible to run checks on people who enter the country without documents or with falsified papers. Any government has to be concerned to make sure, for example, that it does not let violent criminals, or those suspected of war crimes or crimes against humanity in other countries, loose in the community. Long periods of mandatory detention, however, go well beyond this, and Australia is the only country that institutes such a regime.

Considering specifically the processing of asylum seekers outside Australia under the "Pacific Solution" — yet paid for by the Australian government — the humanitarian argument loses plausibility. On the contrary, this was driven in part by instrumental reasoning: statistics showed that, in general, a higher percentage of asylum seekers were granted refugee status under Australia's domestic rules than were granted that status under UNHCR rules (Guardian Unlimited 2001). Also, access to Australian courts complicated and prolonged the process. Most importantly, although Australia would agree to take some of those deemed legitimate refugees, other countries would have to pitch in and take their share. Asylum seekers trying to enter Australia would be treated, then, as if they were a problem for and responsibility of the world community, rather than a problem for and responsibility of the Australian nation (see, e.g., Howard 2001). Through this maneuver, and supported by hastily constructed legislation that included excision of islands and territories from Australia's migration zone, Australia could legally act within international law on refugees, while arguably acting outside of its spirit (U.S. Committee for Refugees 2002).

In these respects, government action was "rational" and strategically adept. One major governmental aim was to send a message to people smugglers and would-be refugees that, having made the dangerous, even life-threatening trip to faraway Australia, there was little chance of gaining asylum there. Even worse, asylum seekers would live in detention camps isolated from the rest of the Australian population, possibly for periods of long duration. Detention camps in Australia, surrounded by razor wire and now run by the private security firm Australasian Correctional Management (ACM), although according to government spokespersons "humanitarian" in their treatment of detainees, were inhospitable enough, it was felt, to act as a major deterrent. The terrible scenes emanating from the Woomera (South Australia), Curtain (Western Australia), Baxter (South Australia), Port Hedland (Western Australia), Villawood (Sydney), and Marybyrnong (Melbourne) detention centers from the late 1990s on — attempted and successful suicides, self-mutilation including the sewing up of lips, hunger strikes, rioting and burning of facilities, desperate attempts to escape and, perhaps most potent of all, people laying down in self-dug graves (for vivid accounts of these events, see Tyler 2003) — although embarrassing to the Australian government did nothing to disrupt this commitment to using the detention centers as a deterrent. In the "Pacific Solution," people would not even make it to the Australian mainland — a symbolic message to both asylum seekers and the Australian public.

A second deterrent effect involved the creation of what is known as the Temporary Protection Visa (TPV). This created two classes of refugees: those who had entered lawfully, and those who were unauthorized entries either by sea or by air. The latter category of people are being punished, and political leaders want it to be known, in Australia and abroad, that these people will be punished and treated differently than other refugees (Mares 2002). Many of those who enter without authorization *even if and when* they are granted refugee status will only ever be given TPVs, currently for three years. The supporting legislation, first introduced in 1999 and modified in 2001, sets in stone this two-level approach, with restrictions on the capacity of those with TPVs to travel overseas, to receive social security benefits, to access English classes available for other refugees and recent immigrants, to seek family reunion, or to ever achieve a more permanent residency status or citizenship. There is no guarantee that TPVs will be renewed after they expire, leaving such refugees in a permanent state of uncertainty about their future, and leaving them unable to establish themselves in Australian society. Permanent residence status, citizenship, and family reunion are available for refugees who enter Australia with some kind of visa (Crock and Saul 2002: chap. 7).[4]

The Howard government's response to asylum seekers, as the focus on deterrence would suggest, involved an international dimension, most importantly the call for other states to control the criminal activity of "people smuggling." In this respect, government actions were a strategy for precipitating new regimes of control not just in the states from which asylum seekers have come, but within the region in countries such as Indonesia and Malaysia. (The globetrotting of Australia's Immigration Minister Phillip Ruddock can be seen in this light.) In other words, an action that is so belligerently and apparently "nationalistic" is, at the same time, an action aimed at furthering the cause of global governance (see the global strategy explained in Ruddock 2002).

On the domestic front, a major aim was to convince the Australian public that the national government was doing everything to ensure the integrity of Australia's borders ("Border Control" became the incumbent Howard government's election platform in the 2001 election). In this respect, the Australian response to asylum seekers, like the responses of many European countries (Castles 2002), is related to the legitimation crisis of the nation-state in the period of intensified globalization. In a period that sees the increasing permeability of boundaries, the globalization of economic activity, and the transformed and less publicly visible role of the state in economic and social life, the territorial boundaries of the nation-state become a site for strengthened political action. Through increased policing and surveillance of borders, and by acting swiftly and decisively, a government can be perceived by its people as a *national* government serving the interests of the nation by exercising a form of control over the global environment. More cynically, by exacerbating fears that the world is unruly, with images of floods of refugees headed for a country's shores, governments can achieve a form of legitimacy by being seen to have the capacity to resolve looming national "crises." In November 1999, in the buildup to the *MV Tampa* affair, Phillip Ruddock claimed on national media programs that 10,000 asylum seekers were ready to leave the Middle East for Australia (ABC Online 1999).

During the *MV Tampa* crisis, many Australians praised Howard's resolute stance. Howard was admired for his strength in dealing with the situation and his refusal to back down from his promise that he would never let the asylum seekers on the *MV Tampa* land in Australia (Ministerial Statements 2001). Howard's popularity surged almost overnight, and it was widely accepted among commentators that his perceived strength turned his electoral fortunes around (Mares 2002; Marr and Wilkinson 2003). Many claim that it won him the election when, in the months leading up to that August, Kim Beazley's Labor was ahead in the polls and headed for victory.

But what of the emotional dynamics involved in reactions to asylum seekers? The vehemence with which, in recent times, asylum seekers have been denigrated by government ministers and officials, and by members of the Australian public, suggests that there are other less than rational layers to the perception of asylum seekers, and to their treatment. There has been, for example, a deliberate process of dehumanizing and demonization involved.

Queue jumpers, potential terrorists, people willing to sacrifice their own children: these labels and claims, made by Australian political leaders about the motives and actions of desperate people, undermined the humanity of asylum seekers and directed sympathy away from them from the late 1980s onward. Members of the Hawke and Keating governments made disparaging comments about Cambodian asylum seekers who began arriving in boats in 1989, claiming that they were "economic migrants" and jumping the queue (Crock and Saul 2002: 31; McMaster 2001: 73–75). These forms of disparagement intensified under the Howard government, and moved to vilification.

In early October 2001, in the heat of the election campaign, Prime Minister Howard, Minister for Immigration Phillip Ruddock, and Defence Minister Peter Reith all claimed that asylum seekers on board the *Olong*, a 25-meter wooden-hulled boat carrying 223 (referred to by government officials as Suspected Illegal Entry Vessel 4 [SIEV IV]), had thrown their own children overboard in an attempt to secure entry into Australia. What kind of people, it was rhetorically asked, would risk the lives of their own children? Howard told radio listeners that "I certainly don't want people of that type in Australia, I really don't" (quoted in Mares 2002: 135). The claims involved in what came to be known as the "Children Overboard Affair" turned out to be false, and controversy remains over what the Prime Minister and others knew about the actual circumstances surrounding the supposed events. A major parliamentary report accused the government of manipulating information, and even deceiving the public in order to present asylum seekers in the worst possible light (Senate Select Committee on a Certain Maritime Incident 2002; for an excellent account of this whole incident, see Marr and Wilkinson 2003). Again, part of this can be attributed to cynical political calculation and an exercise in public relations control.

Others documented the lack of sympathy shown by Immigration Minister Ruddock and other leaders in the face of tales of abuses in detention camps, and in particular of the sufferings of children. In one incident, noted by political commentator Robert Manne (2001), Ruddock repeatedly referred to a young Iranian boy being held in a detention camp as "it" rather than as "he" or by his first name. The boy, Shayan Badraie, during prolonged detention, and after witnessing the attempted suicide and self-mutilation of inmates, had retreated into an almost catatonic state, refusing to eat, drink, or speak. His story had been aired nationally on the ABC's *Four Corners* program, and caused such public controversy that Ruddock responded a few nights later in an interview on the ABC's *7.30 Report*. During the interview, Ruddock made the extraordinary claim that the boy's trauma might be related less to the events of his period in detention than to his being the stepson rather than the biological son of his mother (ABC Online 2001).[5]

In the recent parliamentary report on the "Children Overboard Affair," one witness, who was involved in producing images of the Australian Navy's interception of asylum seeker boats, claimed he was told by the Minister for Defence's media advisor not to produce any images that would "humanize" or "personalize" asylum seekers. All such information and imagery was tightly controlled by the Defence Minister. Members of the Navy were not permitted to speak about any details of the operation unless given permission by the Minister, not even if incorrect information needed to be corrected. This was a crucial factor in the "Children Overboard Affair" and the deception of the Australian public by Minister Reith (Senate Select Committee on a Certain Maritime Incident 2002: 22–25).

A large part of politics involves the systematic organization of enmities, hatreds, and sympathies. As the Australian political scientist Alan Davies once put it, political leaders are like sculptors, and their medium is public emotion (Davies 1980: 293). The examples cited above illustrate how government, through action and language, directed sympathy away from asylum seekers, and in some cases incited suspicion, anger, fear, and even hatred of them, accusing them of being guilty of greedily trying to take the place of "patient," "legitimate" refugees. The Australian public, with the exception of some public figures and groups of concerned citizens who have consistently protested against the vilification and harsh treatment of asylum seekers, has generally been receptive to such messages and has agreed with the government's approach. At the edges of that support were even harder sentiments expressed on the street and on talk-back radio. Some people suggested that the boats should be shot out of the water.

Although it manipulated public emotions, the Howard government did not create them. There seems little doubt that Australians have been for some time receptive to appeals to security and border protection (Mackay 2001), and this only intensified after the events of September 11. When Mick, the Vietnam veteran discussed in earlier chapters, was recently interviewed he reflected that no one, including himself, wanted the refugees from the *MV Tampa* and the other boats to be allowed into Australia:

> You can't just turn them out to sea of course but I personally, and anyone I speak to, doesn't want them here. And I know there's a lot of do-gooders and everyone doesn't have the same opinion. But I've never met anyone — I don't bring up the subject, I'm not a political person — but I've never heard of anyone that wants them here. Now whether on telly there is? But I'd say, as I said, hundreds of people I've spoken to, vets, their wives, no one's ever said they should be here. I don't know whether you should put kids away. The detention centers in Woomera appear not to be that bad to me. I don't really know what they expect. I mean you can't, oh I don't know. I think they've got to stop it before it gets here.

Mick was not an unsympathetic or especially angry man, nor was he someone particularly threatened by "otherness." For many years he had worked doggedly and without pay to look after his fellow veterans. He had worked with Vietnamese refugees in Australia, and had felt for them when he saw that they were being exploited and lived in poverty. In recent years he had visited Vietnam many times and had developed strong links with families and communities there. He did, however, have a particular concern with the impact of Muslim communities in Australia. In this he reflected the climate of prejudice against Muslims that has been most recently exacerbated by the September 11 attacks, but which was evident in Australia in the 1980s. He felt that Muslims were "in a hell of a conflict" with Christians, and from this perspective he could not "see why we need that many Muslims." That was just asking for trouble, in his view. He did not care about color or other markers of ethnicity — people from Asia, Europe, or Africa were all welcome to come to Australia. But he felt that the Muslims who came to Australia, although they seemed to be attracted by Australia's freedom, wanted to change the society around to suit themselves. They would not leave it the way that it was.

In Mick's mind the "illegal immigrant" and the Muslim had become fused into the one symbolic threat to the nation. If you let too many Muslims into the country, they would try to change the best things about it, such as its love of freedom. Other people that I have interviewed have expressed similar sentiments. Perhaps the most telling remarks of John and Eddie, the council workers discussed at the beginning of this chapter, were about their complete lack of trust in the new Iraqi Muslim communities who now live alongside them in their rural town. Albanian and Turkish Muslims have long lived in their town, and apart from typical expressions of xenophobia and casual racism, one is not left with the impression that these Muslims have exercised the minds of anyone terribly much. With the recent predominantly Muslim asylum seekers however, the distrust is palpable. Wayne, the mechanic discussed in earlier chapters, works in an area with a significant Muslim population. He expressed this complete distrust and this complete separation of lives:

> No one really trusts [them] and this is before September 11. No one really trusted them simply because there was no respect. They expect everything for nothing and they'll never go out of their way to help you or do anything. Like if they saw someone fall over in the footpath right next to them, they wouldn't even stop, wouldn't even blink. So they'd just keep walking. And since that time, since that American thing it's probably got worse round here. People just don't, they just switch off on it now. Rather than yelling in the street and all the rest of it they just ignore them. To the point where I've seen you have these little rear end accidents or something in the street and people just ignore them. If it's them in the car they'll go and just keep driving. It's actually to that point, you think that's not really that good.

The Howard government's response to the *MV Tampa* found overwhelming support among the Australian population. In some widely published national polls, more than 75 percent of those interviewed agreed with his actions. One Roy Morgan Poll, comparing attitudes in Australia, New Zealand, the U.S., and the U.K., published in the *Bulletin* (September 25, 2001) found that between 1979 and 2001 Australians had shifted from 53 percent support for accepting boat people (at that time from Indochina) to only 20 percent in September 2001, with 68 percent saying that they should be put back to sea.[6] Even after a Federal Court ruled that the government's actions for detaining people on the *MV Tampa* were unlawful, and ordered that the boat people on the *MV Tampa* be returned to the Australian mainland (later overturned on appeal by a Full Bench of the Federal Court), 76 percent of people said that they should not be returned to the mainland, and only 19 percent said that they should. In the same poll, 65 percent of Australians felt that the Australian government was, overall, doing a good job in handling the refugee problem (23 percent answered very good, 42 percent answered fairly good). When asked if they approved or disapproved of the way that Howard was handling the refugee problem, 70 percent said they approved (Roy Morgan Research 2001).

It is difficult to know from such polls exactly why people were so supportive of the government's actions, and why they were so vehemently opposed to the landing of the asylum seekers from the *MV Tampa* or other boats. There may have been many reasons. Some may have been influenced by the question of supposed "illegality," since many, including political leaders, have repeatedly referred to asylum seekers as illegal immigrants. Because they were "illegal," they should be treated the same as others who have broken the law: either detained, or since they were not Australian citizens, sent away. It hardly matters that asylum seekers who present themselves to Australian officials on arrival are not breaking any laws. The "illegal" label has stuck, despite attempts by human rights advocates to clarify the mistake. A second reason may have been the perception that these people were taking the place of other already legitimately recognized refugees who were waiting in camps or in other places before they could legally enter Australia. There, a zero sum mentality, explicitly fostered by the government's unwavering position on a strict yearly intake of refugees, might lead some people to object to "queue jumpers" on moral grounds.

Others, like Mick, seemed to believe that controlling asylum seekers would help to contain the growth of Muslim communities, and reduce the threat of acts of terror, in Australia.

In the Morgan Poll just discussed, it was noted that the sorts of things people said when they felt that the refugees from the boats should not be allowed in were that the refugees were trying to enter by the "back door" and that they should "join the queue." Some felt that they would worsen the already high unemployment rate. After September 11, the poll noted, there were new attitudes, including: "Look what happened today in America. We don't know who they are and they are a violent race"; and "They are fanatical people."

Control of asylum seekers has been most cogently argued as a sovereignty issue. This is evident enough in the language of the Howard government and other governments before it. Many ordinary Australians say the same sort of thing. Controlling the flow of asylum seekers is an attempt to control national space. For many people, the nation operates as a key form of enclosure, through which they are able to view and negotiate with the rest of the world. Globalization has thrown this key function of the nation as an imagined community into doubt. When globalization is perceived as a threat, as anything goes, as loss of control over one's place, the border becomes a crucial zone of defense. In this respect, the militarization of the issue is understandable.

Although the Australian Defence Forces (ADF) had been involved in border protection and surveillance since the late 1980s, this had typically been in a supportive role. Beginning with the *MV Tampa* crisis, the ADF was directed by the government to take the leading role in detecting and repelling asylum seekers. The initial military campaign was known as Operation

Relex. This also involved a shift in approach. Where previously the ADF had played a supportive role in detecting unauthorized boats in Australian waters and then guiding them to Australian ports, under Operation Relex the ADF adopted a "forward defensive strategy" of detecting and deterring boats before they entered Australian waters (Senate Select Committee on a Certain Maritime Incident 2002: chap. 2). By taking over from nonmilitary organizations like Coastwatch, and organized under a centralized government command — the People Smuggling Taskforce — the protection of the borders from unauthorized boats was recast as a matter of national defense. Symbolically, it became difficult to separate the arrival of boats from the threat of invasion or, after September 11, from the threat of terrorism.

When Wayne was asked recently about the role of defense, he commented that the main task for Australian defense forces should be to protect Australian borders from asylum seekers, or "illegal immigrants" as he called them: "Defense, if anything they should be just defending the boundary of the country against illegal immigrants. That's all they've got to do." Immigration was high on his agenda of national concerns:

Immigration. I think we need to screen the people better. If they haven't got any sort of skill and they're just coming in and bludging, no go. And that covers all the boat loads of people that try to get in all the time. Zero tolerance on that sort of stuff. Because you can only be nice to so many people and then we all go broke in the process.

That last comment "you can only be nice to so many people and then we all go broke in the process" has been echoed by many Australians. Refugees and asylum seekers, often grouped into the one category, are frequently seen as unwelcome new visitors at the national table where the food being handed out is meager. In a relatively affluent and peaceful society such as Australia, callers to talk-back radio at the height of the MV *Tampa* crisis claimed that we simply could not let the boat people in, no matter how desperate they were, because our health and other social services were already at a breaking point.

Sandra, a middle-aged librarian of predominantly liberal predisposition, when I interviewed her in the middle of 2003, felt some concern about the apparent lack of humanitarianism in detention camps for asylum seekers, but nevertheless felt that the government was doing the right thing in "stemming the tide." Even her concern about the camps was tempered by a suspicion that it was a bit of a media beat-up. As she explained, governments had to do something to stop the numbers of people trying to enter Australia, as our social system and system of welfare simply could not cope. Part of the background to this argument was Sandra's observation of the poor state of public education, housing, health, and welfare services in her regional area.

In this respect, the actions of governments from the 1980s onward, in paring back the key institutions of social democracy, have helped to create a climate of intolerance for outsiders who might otherwise, and in more propitious times, excite the sympathies of Australians. But I think that the issue runs even deeper. There is something about the perception of asylum seekers that appears to unite the well-off and those really feeling the brunt of Australia's restructuring. It is reflected in the apparent lack of sympathy for the wretched of the earth among the majority of Australians, and even in the vilification of asylum seekers. Psychoanalysts suggest that one important way of containing anxiety is to project fears related to things one cannot control onto things that one believes one can control and manipulate. What, we may ask, is the psychological load that asylum seekers have been forced to bear by those seeking to repel them?

In the west, anxieties about globalization are being played out through reactions to asylum seekers, and these are given a particular inflection by Australians. Bob, a Vietnam veteran in his seventies who was in fact very supportive of refugees, made a telling remark when asked what was distinctive about Australia: he said that one of the very good things about Australia is its distance from everywhere else. Bob felt that we were lucky to be out of the line of fire of the major conflicts in the Northern Hemisphere:

> I like our remoteness from the world. Even though the world is now, we're part of the world, we still have that space and distance which just takes us away. It's a step away from the world's problems. So often, it'll probably change here, but so often when people are gunning or shooting, in terms of not just using guns, but having cracks at each other, it always seems to be across that Northern Hemisphere. You don't see much involvement in New Zealand or Australia. The remoteness — I do like that. It's always been good for Australia in many ways. It's been a disadvantage in many ways, but we're now, unfortunately it's going to get closer as we get down the track.

Over the years I have heard many people say many such things. At the height of fears about a nuclear holocaust in the 1980s, people in Australia took comfort in living some distance away from the major sites of direct confrontation. To the extent that fears were raised, they were concerned by things such as the secret operations of American bases in Australia, for example the one at Pine Gap, that might draw Australia into a nuclear conflict.

This is one of Australia's oldest cultural habits: viewing the outside world as a threat and a danger, measured against the promise of paradise within. The sense of paradise and plenty has also given rise to the fear of envy, especially from the Asian world, which is Australia's closest neighbor, and has been expressed in the periodic outburst of invasion fears. The feeling of being distant from the main sites of real action is in itself double-sided. First is the attitude just cited, that it is good to have distance between Australia and the rest of the world, not just for security reasons, but for reasons of cultural development. (In earlier times, this included the New World ideology that Australia was a social laboratory where new things could be tried out without the hindrance of Old World history and tradition.) But this is coupled with the fantasy that all that is dangerous is *out there*, and that if Australians stay where they are, and can continue to keep the rest of the world at a distance, then they are safe from the world.

In the present, Australians, who live in a relatively peaceful society and one characterized by a remarkable level of political calm, view a more brutal and violent world every night on their televisions, and in real time. There is a sense in which unauthorized asylum seekers are perceived as bringing all of the death and destruction viewed on Australian television screens, beamed in from other places, into Australia. Although the images are haunting, one can feel compelled to block them out. One can feel bombarded and even angry at being exposed to such images that disturb the conduct of ordinary life. One can refuse to look or turn off the television.

People speak of compassion fatigue (Cohen 2001). But there is also the way that such media exposure, decontextualized as images of insane conflict, allows people to perceive these events — governmental brutality, wars, acts of genocide, and persecution — as somehow inherently related to the types of people who engage in them, with their "ancient tribal hatreds" and their backwardness. Lacking a knowledge of the complexities of the political, economic, and social situations in which those actions and events occur — complexities typically lacking in a great deal of media exposure — stereotypes of barbarity fill the gap. This allows for a fantasy to emerge that decrees that peace at home can only be maintained by keeping those sorts of "barbaric" people out.

When, for example, it had been revealed that the people picked up by the MV Tampa were mainly Afghans at the same time that the link was being established between Afghanistan, the Taliban, and Al-Qaeda in the wake of September 11, some Australians believed that the MV Tampa Afghans were tarred by the same brush, despite the fact that they were obviously fleeing from the Taliban regime. In the aftermath of September 11, even Prime Minister Howard, like his Defence Minister Peter Reith on many occasions before him, suggested that we could not be certain that terrorists were not among the asylum seekers (Mares 2002: 134; Marr and Wilkinson 2003: 151, 198, 280–281).

Globalization for those in the west involves a heightened awareness of the terrible plight of others in desperate situations. Mass communications and widespread international travel make this awareness unavoidable. The recognition that westerners have it so good by comparison does not necessarily lead to a generous approach to those less well off. In fact, it frequently leads to the opposite, to the fear of envy. The gross inequality of the world, which many claim has been exacerbated by economic globalization (see, e.g., Sklair 2001), leads to a belief that the underprivileged of the world want what "we" have and will do everything that they can to get it. As part of the same psychologically charged process, there is also fear that "we," the privileged, will sink into the same mire if "we" show signs of generosity toward the teeming millions of the underprivileged. There is fear that "they" will overwhelm "us." There is a willingness to believe that others are only out to exploit "us" (the term "economic refugees" is especially poignant in Australia given that many of Australia's settlers, throughout its history, have left their homelands in search of economic and social improvement).

It is not especially helpful to argue that these reactions are simply a recurrence of the invasion fears that have long haunted the Australian imagination (e.g., see McMaster 2001). They are not necessarily racist either, in any obvious sense. They are far more specifically situated fears and anxieties about the nature of a globalized world and perceived threats to national sovereignty, national borders, and, in the end, national identity that are shared by many people in countries throughout the world. They are fears about the loss of the things people value about Australia — the openness, friendliness, and civil peace. They reflect a far more interconnected world, and the understanding that those interconnections have brought home to others in less privileged circumstances that there are places of privilege, like Australia, where people live far safer, more economically certain and freer lives. The fear is related to the knowledge of what others know, and this in turn inspires guilt and defenses against it. We know that we depend on others for our own prosperity, but we know also that if we allow those others to enjoy our privileges this will inevitably lead to a lowering of the standards that we enjoy.

In this situation, the adherence to strict and unforgiving rules can act as a calming influence, and dampen moral sensibilities, the very rationality of the language concealing the depth of emotion and the forms of guilt that have to be kept at bay. Here is Carol, first introduced in Chapter Three, who from her reading of popular history and novels is well aware of the terrible plight of asylum seekers from the Middle East and Afghanistan, trying to grapple with the way that we treat such people in contemporary Australia:

[What do you think of the refugees from there?] Oh that's so sad too. I do believe that perhaps we should accept them but really they've got to come in the right way. There's got to be rules and regulations, and a correct way of doing things. We'd have the country flooded with them. They'll be all coming from everywhere otherwise if we don't put our foot down and have some sort of rules and regulations. But I feel for them. I mean if they're brave enough to uproot themselves from their own countries like that. They're often quite well educated people that are doing it. They must be desperate.

Now on the verge of retirement, Carol still lives in a regional city and heads, together with her husband, a large and thriving business. Carol is acutely aware not only of her own wealth and privilege (which causes her some embarrassment) but also of the comparative privileges of living in Australia:

Our economy is rather good generally you know. Compared to a lot of other countries I think we are far better off, wealthwise. Even our poor aren't as poor as you see elsewhere. You don't see the beggars in the streets like you do in say Italy and Greece. Even in France or Paris, beggars everywhere. Like gypsies fleecing you. We don't seem to have a lot of that.

She has firsthand experience of asylum seekers, living near a settlement (this was not a detention camp) set up by the government to receive Kosovars during the crisis of 1999. Australia accepted Kosovars on temporary protection visas, but then sent them back, under considerable protest from many of them, once the immediate conflict was over:

A lot of them were quite well educated people. A few of them have managed to stay. Their circumstances lent itself to being accepted at the time. But most of them were sent back and they had to reapply through the correct channels. I don't know whether they get preference by doing it that way, but a lot of them had nothing to go back to either. Their homes were gone. Very hard decision. I would hate to be John Howard or whoever makes all the decisions on this. Sending people back to nothing. But you've got to put your foot down and you've got to make a decision and stick by it and have your rules. I believe in rules. If a group make up their mind about something, it's got to be accepted. If the majority agree everybody's got to go along with it, I do wholeheartedly believe.

Carol's position is ambivalent, although she takes comfort in the fact that the "majority" has decided and therefore everybody has to abide by the rules. A more interconnected world also means that people have to find new ways to measure out their sympathy. Rules and regulations, the wishes of the majority, can allow one to calibrate one's sympathies in relation to collective sympathies.

The Howard government's position, on the other hand, was far from ambivalent. While engaging in subtle and not-so-subtle acts of vilification of asylum seekers, it hid its repressive actions behind legality, changing legislation in order to give the appearance that it was behaving in a legal-rational manner. When it was clear that elements of its own legal-rational system would impede government efforts to deal with asylum seekers in a new way in the post-*MV Tampa* era, it just went on shifting the goalposts. In November 2003, a small boat carrying 15 Kurdish asylum seekers entered Australian waters, prompting the Howard government to retrospectivley excise more than four thousand small islands, including Melville Island where the asylum seekers had first landed, from Australia's migration zone.[7]

One of the possible virtues of a close examination of a region or society is that it will shed light on the complex ways that new global realities get refracted through cultures and places that have particular histories of formation, traditions and characteristics, and particular positions within the global economy and global power relations (Appadurai 1996; Paolini 1999; Hoogvelt 2001). The major features of globalization have been explored here through an overview of the history and development of Australian society.

The burgeoning literature on globalization often speaks in an abstract voice. In this book I have been as concerned to think through Australians' perceptions of the changes to their lives and identities that can be attributed to the processes of globalization, as I was to explain the full extent of these changes. I hope that these Australian voices enliven and enrich the more abstract and theoretical work involved in understanding globalization, in Australia and elsewhere. There are, of course, other ways to look at these changes that we think of as globalization. What people think and believe, though it is an important part of reality, is not the whole of reality or the whole of explanation.

I am left with the seeming paradox of a persisting Australian national reality and political culture in the context of the opening up of society through intensifying globalization. But it is only a paradox if one is convinced by the argument that national identity has been, or is being, crushed under the wheels of globalization. I do not think that it has or is, in Australia or in many other places. National identity is for many people a buffer against a world that often seems unruly, and sometimes simply frightening. Nations are important forms of closure from within which people negotiate their relationship with the rest of the world. But a nation is not only a haven. For many people it is a positive and ongoing project, linking the past with the present and future. For many, national identity provides an important narrative framework for their lives, and even helps to give their lives broader meaning.

Contemporary Australia is, no doubt, a complex place. At times and in places, it is uneasy and uncertain. As I have shown in this book, Australians have experienced massive changes since the Second World War. The reorientation of the state and the shift to more market-oriented economic relations; the loosening of economic controls and more open and diverse trading relations; the ethnic diversification of the population and the rise of multiculturalism; the reopening of settler/indigenous conflicts and the new forms of nationalism this has stimulated; revolutions in transport and communication and the new influences and horizons these have stimulated — all of these have made Australia a very different and more global place than it was previously. And yet, the concerns, the debates, and the public responses inspired by globalizing processes are marked by Australian history and Australian realities. Although it is not true for everyone, for many Australians the nation still operates as an important framework, and moral community, through which they argue, explain, understand, and feel these new realities. Even multiculturalism, that byword for one important cultural aspect of globalization, is, as I showed in Chapter Three, very much an Australian version of that global phenomenon.

In a context of economic internationalization, large-scale movement of peoples including asylum seekers, and the rise of global terror networks, Australians are constantly reminded that borders can and will be penetrated, and that the world will continue to come in, pervade, and reshape bounded national space. It seems unlikely that any of these things will lessen in intensity in the future. One can only hope to be proven wrong in the case of global terror. It is also to be hoped that Australians find new ways to understand and deal with the global problem of asylum seekers, and that this can in the future be distinguished from the issues of national security, and of the growing importance of Muslim communities in Australia.

The response to asylum seekers has unnerved many in the country. I spent little time in Chapter Five explaining the feelings and activities of those Australians who have been appalled by Australia's recent reaction to asylum seekers, to ongoing detention, to turning boats away, and to the new strategy of offshore processing known as the "Pacific Solution." Churches, trade unions, support groups, and individual citizens have staged protests, written letters to newspapers and political leaders, raised funds, visited and corresponded with asylum seekers, and set up networks to receive refugees on the run from authorities. While the opposition has been in the minority, it has been a passionate minority. It is finding expression at the political level. Apart from protest and opposition from the Greens and the Democrats, there are now people within the Australian Labor Party calling for a reassessment of the whole approach to dealing with asylum seekers, including those elements, like mandatory detention, that the party in government and opposition had previously supported. No doubt such opposition exists in the National and Liberal parties, although it has been stifled by calls for strength and unity.

There is evidence in such passionate defense of the rights of asylum seekers of a moral sensibility that is less bounded by national belonging (Brett 2003: 216). Human rights are global rights. On the other hand, many of the most ardent supporters of the rights of asylum seekers also argue that they are, in fact, giving voice to the "true" Australian spirit of compassion and tolerance. They love and care for their nation just as much as those who claim they are only defending their nation's sovereignty against "illegals."

Australians in the recent past have found ways to handle and celebrate diversity as great as that now represented by Muslim communities, including those from the Middle East. The public commitment to multiculturalism, despite sometimes vociferous opposition, has held since the 1970s. The current panic about Muslims, in any case, should not be exaggerated. It has not been condoned in any significant way at the political level, where governments and opposition parties have been quick to reassure Muslim leaders and communities that they are as welcome in Australia as any other Australian.

Increasingly, Australia's domestic issues must be handled with an eye to places outside Australia. This is the case not only with issues such as the state's handling of interest rates, the management of trade and related policies, public spending and debt, taxation, inflation, labor costs, unemployment, and industrial relations more generally, but also with issues such as the management of race relations. Many recognized this, for example, when Hanson and her One Nation Party started making reactionary noises about the "Asianization" of Australia, and about Australia's policies on race and indigenous issues more generally.

Australia's important cultural, trade, economic, and security links with Asian countries in the region could be easily exposed and undermined by perceptions of Australia as anti-Asian, or as retreating into its past as a white Australia. Similarly, given its long colonial history, Australia has had to be careful not to be seen as reinventing its colonial role by becoming, in President Bush's unfortunate words, a sheriff in the Asia-Pacific region.

Information that, in the past, would leak out of the country over months, perhaps modified and sanitized in diplomatic reports, is now received almost instantaneously, and is fed back to a nervous Australian public that realizes how closely its well-being is now tied to perceptions in its own region, and the world beyond.

This book has been written in the shadow of the "war on terror" — a war that Australia, as an ally of the U.S. and Britain, has taken on as its own. Australia's recent involvement in the Gulf War, limited as it was, has meant that Australia has committed itself to a role in ensuring global security. As in the past, it has seen its own national interests as intrinsically bound with broader international trends and events. As I noted in the introduction of this book, Australia has always had to keep one eye firmly fixed on the outside world. Whether through its actions Australia contributes to furthering global security remains to be seen. At the same time, its recent commitments have pulled against other old cultural habits.

Australians know that they belong to a small, or at the very best medium, power. We know that our influence on the rest of the world is not great. Distance and spatial proximity still matter, despite the massive changes in transport and communications from the latter part of the twentieth century. These facts give rise to different approaches to understanding our relationship to the rest of the world, and in particular to the Northern

Hemisphere. Some like Bob — and there are many others — wish that Australians could remember to keep their heads down, below the parapet so to speak. Bob's comments (quoted in the last chapter) indicate the persistence of an older spatial understanding of Australia as an island continent far removed from the conflicts of the Old World, even in this age of globalization and the shrinking of distance. The Howard government's commitment of troops to Iraq, mostly for surveillance, intelligence, and support, divided the Australian population, with some of the largest demonstrations seen on city streets since the Vietnam War. It has become a major political issue in the lead up to the next federal election. The new Labor opposition leader, Mark Latham, is promising to bring the troops back home by Christmas. He, like many others, believes that the situation in Iraq is becoming a debacle. We had no right to get involved, he has argued, and his claim is echoed by many other Australians publicly and in private. The failure to find Weapons of Mass Destruction only adds further to the belief that Australia's involvement was wrong. The Howard government faces the possible wrath of the people because of the perception that its actions in Iraq, and in highlighting Australia's agreement with U.S. foreign policy, has increased the threat of terrorist acts in Australia or against Australians outside the country. Howard and his government may have offended Australians' deep cultural habit of seeing their country as a safe and distant haven from the conflicts and dangers of the Old World. The Australian forces, Latham argues, need to be devoted to protecting Australian interests in our own immediate region. Our intelligence capacities should be devoted to combating terrorism closer to home, in South-East Asia and on Australian soil. The notion of the preemptive strike is dead. The alliance with the U.S., he argues, should be returned to a more equal footing.[1] His comments, especially those concerning the nature of the alliance, have led to a public rebuke from the U.S. State Department, which described them as "neither well informed nor well based."[2]

The Howard government has staked much on the importance of the alliance with the U.S. Its view has been that, in a world with only one superpower, it is in Australia's immediate and long-term interests to do everything to strengthen ties with that superpower, which is, afterall, a traditional ally (at least since the Second World War). Australians are pulled in different directions, at once feeling the force of the argument about needing the protection of the one great power, and sensing that there might be some economic benefit to be had from closer ties with the U.S., but at the same time feeling that Australian sovereignty is being undermined by following too closely American aims in world politics. The Labor Opposition is banking on people's feeling of national independence finally winning out.

Such arguments do not reflect a retreat from the implications of globalization. Latham is well aware of such implications for Australia.[3] Instead, it is an assertion of Australian interests and sovereignty in the context of globalization. Nobody of any real public importance in Australia is suggesting that Australia should retreat from the world and disengage from cooperation with other countries. As I argued in Chapter One, globalization has entailed the rise of new forms of governance that reach beyond the nation-state, to regions, and to the globe. It is clear that Australian interests can only be served by cooperating in transnational forums — but on our own terms.

Notes

1 Howard and members of his government have emphasized this point since the late 1990s. See, for example, Howard's ministerial statement to parliament at the height of the *MV Tampa* crisis, on August 29, 2001 (Ministerial Statements 2001).

ONE: GLOBALIZING AUSTRALIA

1 For the transformation of Australia's trade figures after the Second World War, see Fagan and Webber (1994: chap. 3). They point out that, although Australia continued after 1950 to receive the bulk of its foreign investment from Britain, trade with Britain declined dramatically. In 1950–1951, Britain purchased about one-third of Australia's exports, but by 1975–1976, it had fallen to four percent. In the same period, Japan's purchasing of Australian exports increased from about six percent to 33 percent (Fagan and Webber 1994: 50–51).

2 As Capling (2001: 1) points out, "in 1997 Australia's most important trade partner, Japan, accounted for only 20 percent of its exports and just under 14 percent of its imports. By contrast, Canada conducts 80 percent of its two-way trade with its biggest trade partner, the United States."

3 The Harvester Judgement, adjudicated by the president of the Commonwealth Conciliation and Arbitration Court Judge H. B. Higgins in 1907, defined the family wage as sufficient for a man, his wife, and three children to live in "frugal comfort." This definition concerned male wages only. "Fair and reasonable" female wages would be less, Higgins noted,

because in most cases women did not have to support a family. See Castles (1994); Jamrozik (1994).

4 Protection was not simply the "dead weight" of a "fearful and defensive Australia" that had "built walls to protect itself against the challenge of the outside world," resulting in Australia protecting "itself against the recognition and utilisation of opportunity," to quote from Ross Garnaut's influential report *Australia and the Northeast Asian Ascendency* (Garnaut 1989: 1). The idea, promoted by some critics in the 1980s and 1990s, that the era of protection gave Australians a false sense of security in the world, is an exaggeration (see Kelly 1992; for a critique of Kelly's position, see Maddox 1998).

TWO: GLOBALIZATION, NATIONAL BELONGING, AND NATIONAL IDENTITY

1 "I have twenty-seven years of exile behind me, and my spiritual compatriots are Proust, Sartre, Beckett. Only I am still convinced that one must have compatriots in village and city streets if the spiritual ones are to be fully enjoyed, and that a cultural internationalism thrives well only in the soil of national security... One must have a home in order not to need it, just as in thinking one must have mastery of the field of formal logic in order to proceed beyond it to more fertile regions of the mind" (Améry 1986: 46).

FOUR: THE DILEMMAS OF SETTLER/INDIGENOUS RELATIONS

1 As he points out (p. 218), he drew his four categories from those used by D. K. Fieldhouse in *The Colonial Empires: A Comparative Survey from the Eighteenth Century*.

2 Alfred Deakin, Commonwealth Parliamentary Debates, House of Representatives, September 12, 1901, p. 4805.

3 The organization was originally called the Federal Council for the Advancement of Aborigines (FCAA). It changed its name to FCAATSI in 1964.

4 Commonwealth Parliamentary Debates, House of Representatives, May 16–17 (overnight sitting), 1985, p. 2635.

5 Commonwealth Parliamentary Debates, House of Representatives, May 20, 1985, pp. 2691–2693.

6 Commonwealth Parliamentary Debates, House of Representatives, May 20, 1985, p. 2704.
7 The letter was published in The Australian, March 27, 1985, and was quoted by Everingham, Commonwealth Parliamentary Debates, House of Representatives, May 20, 1985, p. 2691.

FIVE: ASYLUM SEEKERS: THE POLITICS OF SYMPATHY AND THE EXPERIENCE OF GLOBALIZATION

1 The estimate is AUS 500 million dollars (Senate Select Committee on a Certain Maritime Incident 2002).
2 Twelve arrived by plane; see Robert Manne, "A Stained Chapter in Our History," The Age, Opinion, July 22, 2002, p. 11.
3 Unauthorized Arrivals by Air and Sea, Fact Sheet no. 74, Department of Immigration and Multicultural and Indigenous Affairs, Revised July 22, 2002 (cited in Senate Select Committee on a Certain Maritime Incident 2002: 291).
4 The Howard government was prepared to go to extraordinary lengths to police this, as exemplified by the famous case of Ahmed Alzalimi, who lost his three daughters in the SEIV X disaster in late 2001 where 353 asylum seekers perished after their boat sank on the way from Indonesia to Australia. Alzalimi was not allowed to visit his grieving wife who had survived the sinking and was now back in Indonesia (see Mares 2002: 202). If he chose to do so, the conditions of his temporary visa meant that he would be prevented from reentering Australia.
5 Reading the transcript of the interview, the repeated use of the term "it" when referring to the boy, and the complete refusal on the part of Ruddock to use the boy's name is indeed striking, and disturbing, especially when counterposed to the repeated use of the boy's name by the interviewer. It seems almost as if Ruddock were behaving in a scripted way deliberately designed to avoid humanizing the young boy.
6 For a more complex explanation for the types and levels of support for Indo-Chinese boat people in the late 1970s, see Murray Goot (2001: 825).
7 "New Bid to Repel Asylum Seekers," The Australian, November 5, 2003, p. 1.

1 Comments made in a recent speech to the Lowy Institute in Sydney. An
edited version of the speech appeared in The Age, April 8, 2004, p. 17.
2 Reported in the Sydney Morning Herald, April 13, 2004.
3 He has even written a book about it. See Latham (1998).

Bibliography

ABC Online (1999) "Government Struggles to Stop Flow of Refugees," *PM Program*, Monday, November 15, 1999. Online. Transcript Available http: <http://www.abc.net.au/pm/s66365.htm> (accessed September 18, 2003).

——— (2001) "Phillip Ruddock Interview with Kerry O'Brien," 7:30 *Report*, August 14, 2001. Online. Transcript Available http: <http://www.abc. net.au/7.30/s34619.htm> (accessed July 20, 2003).

Aitkin, D. (1986) "Australian Political Culture," *Australian Cultural History* No. 5: 5–11.

Almond, G.A. (1989) "The Intellectual History of the Civic Culture Concept," in G.A. Almond and S. Verba (eds.), *The Civic Culture Revisited*, Newbury Park, California: Sage, pp. 1–36.

Almond, G.A. and Verba, S. (1963) *The Civic Culture: Political Attitudes and Democracy in Five Nations*, Princeton, New Jersey: Princeton University Press.

Altman, D. (2001) *Global Sex*, Chicago and London: The University of Chicago Press.

Améry, J. (1986) "How Much Home Does a Person Need?," in *At the Mind's Limits: Contemplations By a Survivor on Auschwitz and its Realities*, New York: Schocken Books, pp. 41–61.

Anderson, B. (1983) *Imagined Communities: Reflections on the Origin and Spread of Nationalism*, London: Verso.

——— (1998) "Long-Distance Nationalism" in *The Spectre of Comparisons: Nationalism, Southeast Asia, and the World*, London: Verso, chap. 3.

Appadurai, A. (1996) *Modernity at Large: Cultural Dimensions of Globalization*, Minneapolis/London: University of Minnesota Press.

Assies, W., van der Haar, G. and Hoekema, A. (eds.) (1999) *The Challenge of Diversity: Indigenous Peoples and Reform of the State in Latin America*, Amsterdam: Thela Thesis.

Atkinson, W. (2001) "Not One Iota: the Yorta Yorta Struggle for Land Justice," unpublished PhD thesis, Latrobe University, Melbourne, Australia.

Attwood, B. (2003) *Rights for Aborigines*, Crows Nest, NSW: Allen & Unwin.

Attwood, B. and Markus, A. in collaboration with Edwards, D. and Schilling, K. (1997) *The 1967 Referendum, Or When Aborigines Didn't Get the Vote*, Canberra: Australian Institute of Aboriginal and Torres Strait Islander Studies.

Austin, T. (1997) *Never Trust a Government Man: Northern Territory Aboriginal Policy 1911–1939*, Darwin: Northern Territory University Press.

Australia, Review of Post-Arrival Programs and Services for Migrants (1978) *Migrant Services and Programs: Report of the Review of Post-Arrival Programs and Services for Migrants, May 1978*, Vols. 1 and 2, Canberra: Australian Government Publishing Service.

Australian Bureau of Statistics (2002) *Australia Now. Population: International Migration*. Online. Available http: <http://www.abs.gov.au> (accessed July 7, 2002).

────── (2003) *Year Book Australia 2003*. Online. Available http: <http://www.abs.gov.au> (accessed October 8, 2003)

Australian National Opinion Polls (1985) *Land Rights: Winning Middle Australia — An Attitude and Communications Research Study* (presented to the Department of Aboriginal Affairs, January 1985), Crows Nest, New South Wales: ANOP Market Research — For Government and Industry.

Bandler, F. (1989) *Turning the Tide: A Personal History of the Federal Council for the Advancement of Aborigines and Torres Strait Islanders*, Canberra: Aboriginal Studies Press.

Barwick, D. (1972) "Corandeerk and Cumeroogunga: Pioneers and Policy," in T.S. Epstein and D.H. Penny (eds.), *Opportunity and Response: Case Studies in Economic Development*, London: C. Hurst and Company, pp. 11–69.

Battiste, M. (ed.) (2000) *Reclaiming Indigenous Voice and Vision*, Vancouver: UBC Press.

Bauman, Z. (1997) "The Making and Unmaking of Strangers," in *Postmodernity and its Discontents*, Cambridge: Polity Press, chap. 2.

────── (1998) *Globalization: The Human Consequences*, Cambridge: Polity Press.

────── (2001) *The Individualized Society*, Cambridge: Polity Press.

BBC News (2001a) "Tampa Captain's Tale of Woe," BBC News, Monday, August 27, 2001. Online. Available http: <http://news.bbc.co.uk/hi/english/world/asia-pacific/newsid_15.../1511903.st> (accessed July 22, 2002).

———— (2001b) "Australia Defiant in Refugee Standoff," BBC News, Friday, August 21, 2001. Available http: <http://news.bbc.co.uk/1/hi/world/asia-pacific/15117868.stm> (accessed October 3, 2003).

Beck, U. (1992) Risk Society: Towards a New Modernity, London: Sage.

———— (1997) The Reinvention of Politics: Rethinking Modernity in the Global Social Order, Cambridge: Polity Press.

———— (2000) "The Cosmopolitan Perspective: Sociology of the Second Age of Modernity," British Journal of Sociology 51(1): 79–105.

———— (2002) "The Cosmopolitan Society and its Enemies," Theory, Culture and Society 19(1–2): 17–44.

Beeson, M. and Firth, A. (1998) "Neoliberalism as a Political Rationality: Australian Public Policy Since the 1980s," Journal of Sociology 34(3): 215–229.

Bell, S. and Head, B. (eds.) (1994) State, Economy and Public Policy in Australia, Melbourne: Oxford University Press.

Benhabib, S. (1999) "Civil Society and the Politics of Identity and Difference in a Global Context," in N.J. Smelser and J. Alexander (eds.), Diversity and its Discontents: Cultural Conflict and Common Ground in Contemporary American Society, Princeton, New Jersey: Princeton University Press, pp. 293–312.

Bennett, S. (1989) Aborigines and Political Power, Sydney: Allen & Unwin.

Betts, K. (1988) Ideology and Immigration: Australia 1976 to 1987, Melbourne: Melbourne University Press.

———— (1999) The Great Divide: Immigration Politics in Australia, Sydney: Duffy and Snellgrove.

Blainey, G. (1984) All For Australia, North Ryde: Methuen Haynes.

———— (1985) Triumph of the Nomads: A History of Ancient Australia, revised edn., South Melbourne: Sun Books.

———— (1991) Blainey Eye on Australia: Speeches and Essays of Geoffrey Blainey, Melbourne: Schwartz and Wilkinson.

———— (1994) A Shorter History of Australia, Melbourne: William Heinemann Australia.

Borland, J., Gregory, B. and Sheehan, P. (2001) (eds.) Work Rich, Work Poor: Inequality and Economic Change in Australia, Melbourne: Centre for Strategic Economic Studies, Victoria University.

Boyne, R. (2001) "Cosmopolis and Risk: A Conversation with Ulrich Beck," Theory, Culture and Society 18(4): 47–63.

Braithwaite, J. (2002) "Globalization and Australian Institutions," in G. Brennan and F. Castles (eds.), *Australia Reshaped: 200 Years of Institutional Transformation*, Cambridge: Cambridge University Press, chap. 4.

Brennan, F. (1995) *One Land, One Nation: Mabo — Towards 2001*, St. Lucia, Queensland: University of Queensland Press.

Brett, J. (1992) *Robert Menzies' Forgotten People*, Sydney: Macmillan.

―――― (1996) "Australia," in A. Milner and M. Quilty (eds.), *Australia in Asia: Communities of Thought*, Melbourne: Oxford University Press, pp. 184–202.

―――― (2003) *Australian Liberals and the Moral Middle Class: From Alfred Deakin to John Howard*, Cambridge: Cambridge University Press.

Broome, R. (1994) "Aboriginal Victims and Voyagers, Confronting Frontier Myths," *Journal of Australian Studies* No. 42: 70–77.

Bryan, D. and Rafferty, M. (1999) *The Global Economy in Australia: Global Integration and National Economic Policy*, St. Leonards, New South Wales: Allen & Unwin.

Butlin, N.G., Barnard, A. and Pincus, J.J. (1982) *Government and Capitalism: Public and Private Choice in Twentieth Century Australia*, Sydney: Allen & Unwin.

Campbell, G. and Uhlmann, M. (1995) *Australia Betrayed*, Victoria Park, Western Australia: Foundation Press.

Capling, A. (2001) *Australia and the Global Trade System: From Havana to Seattle*, Cambridge: Cambridge University Press.

Capling, A., Considine, M. and Crozier, M. (1998) *Australian Politics in the Global Era*, South Melbourne: Longman.

Castles, F. (1985) *The Working Class and Welfare: Reflections on the Political Development of the Welfare State in Australia and New Zealand, 1890–1980*, Sydney: Allen & Unwin.

―――― (1994) "'The Wage Earners' Welfare State Revisited: Refurbishing the Established Model of Australian Social Protection, 1983–93," *Australian Journal of Social Issues* 29(2): 120–145.

Castles, S. (2002) "The International Politics of Forced Migration," in L. Panitch and C. Leys (eds.), *Socialist Register 2003, Fighting Identities: Race, Religion and Ethno-Nationalism*, London: The Merlin Press, pp. 172–192.

Castles, S. and Miller, M.J. (1998) *The Age of Migration: International Population Movements in the Modern World*, 2nd edn., London: Macmillan Press.

Castles, S., Cope, B., Kalantzis, M. and Morrissey, M. (1988) *Mistaken Identity: Multiculturalism and the Demise of Nationalism in Australia*, Sydney: Pluto Press.

Catley, B. (1996) *Globalising Australian Capitalism*, Cambridge: Cambridge University Press.

Chesterman, J. (2001a) "Defending Australia's Reputation: How Indigenous Australians Won Civil Rights, Part One," *Australian Historical Studies* 32(116): 20–39.

——— (2001b) "Defending Australia's Reputation: How Indigenous Australians Won Civil Rights, Part Two," *Australian Historical Studies* 32(117): 201–221.

Chesterman, J. and Galligan, B. (1997) *Citizens Without Rights: Aborigines and Australian Citizenship*, Cambridge: Cambridge University Press.

Christie, M.F. (1979) *Aborigines in Colonial Victoria: 1835–86*, Sydney: Sydney University Press.

Cohen, R. (1997) *Global Diasporas: An Introduction*, Seattle: University of Washington Press.

Cohen, R. and Rai, S.M. (2000) "Global Social Movements: Towards a Cosmopolitan Politics," in R. Cohen and S.M. Rai (eds.), *Global Social Movements*, London and New Brunswick, New Jersey: The Athlone Press, pp. 1–17.

Cohen, S. (2001) *States of Denial: Knowing About Atrocities and Suffering*, Cambridge: Polity Press.

Cole, P. (2000) *Philosophies of Exclusion: Liberal Theory and Immigration*, Edinburgh: Edinburgh University Press.

Committee to Advise on Australia's Immigration Policies (1988) *Immigration, A Commitment to Australia: The Report of the Committee to Advise on Australia's Immigration Policies*, Canberra: Australian Government Publishing Service.

Commonwealth of Australia (1991) *Royal Commission into Aboriginal Deaths in Custody, National Reports*, Canberra: Australian Government Publishing Service.

Conley, T. (2001) "The Domestic Politics of Globalisation," *Australian Journal of Political Science* 36(2): 223–246.

Coombs, H.C. (1978) *Kulinma: Listening to Aboriginal Australians*, Canberra: Australian National University Press.

Cope, B. and Kalantzis, M. (2000) *A Place in the Sun: Re-creating the Australian Way of Life*, Sydney: HarperCollins.

Costar, B. (1997) "Electoral Systems," in D. Woodward, A. Parkin and J. Summers (eds.), *Government, Politics, Power and Policy in Australia*, 6th edn., South Melbourne: Longman, pp. 225–239.

Cox, R. (1997) "Economic Globalization and the Limits of Liberal Democracy," in A. McGrew (ed.), *The Transformation of Democracy: Globalization and Territorial Democracy*, Cambridge: Polity Press, pp. 49–72.

Crock, M. and Saul, B. (2002) *Future Seekers: Refugees and the Law in Australia*, Sydney: The Federation Press.

Curr, E.M. (1883) *Recollections of Squatting in Victoria, Then Called the Port Phillip District (from 1841 to 1851)*, Melbourne: G. Robertson.

Curthoys, A. (2002) *Freedom Ride: A Freedom Rider Remembers*, Crows Nest, New South Wales: Allen & Unwin.

Davies, A.F. (1966), *Australian Democracy: An Introduction to the Political System*, 2nd edn., Melbourne: Longmans.

——— (1980) *Skills, Outlooks and Passions: A Psychoanalytic Contribution to the Study of Politics*, Cambridge: Cambridge University Press.

Department of the Prime Minister and Cabinet, Office of Multicultural Affairs (1989) *National Agenda for a Multicultural Australia: Sharing Our Future*, Canberra: Australian Government Publishing Service.

Dilke, C.W. (1872) *Greater Britain: A Record of Travel in English-Speaking Countries During 1866 and 1867*, 6th edn., London: MacMillan and Co.

Dixson, M. (1999) *The Imaginary Australian*, Sydney: UNSW Press.

Dodson, M. (1995) *Native Title Report July 1994–June 1995. Report of the Aboriginal and Torres Strait Islander Social Justice Commissioner to the Minister for Aboriginal and Torres Strait Islander Affairs as required by Section 209 of the Native Title Act 1993*, Sydney: Human Rights and Equal Opportunity Commission.

Dodson, P. (1999) "Lingiari — Until the Chains Are Broken," 4th Annual Vincent Lingiari Memorial Lecture, Friday, August 27, 1999, Mal Nairn Auditorium, Northern Territory University. Reconciliation and Social Justice Library. Online. Available http: <http://www.austlii.edu.au/au/special/ rsjproject/rsjlibrary/car/lingiari/4dodson.html> (accessed November 6, 2003).

Edwards, B. (1994) "Living the Dreaming," in C. Bourke and B. Edwards (eds.), *Aboriginal Australia: An Introductory Reader in Aboriginal Studies*, St. Lucia: University of Queensland Press, chap. 5.

Eggleston, F. (1932) *State Socialism in Victoria*, London: F.S. King & Sons.

——— (1953) "The Australian Nation," in G. Craiger (ed.), *The Australian Way of Life*, London: Heinemann, pp. 1–22.

Emy, H. (1993) *Remaking Australia: The State, the Market and Australia's Future*, St. Leonards: Allen & Unwin.

Evans, M.D.R. and Kelley, J. (2002) *Australian Economy and Society 2001: Education,Work and Welfare*, Sydney: The Federation Press.

Fagan, R.H. and Webber, M. (1994) *Global Restructuring: The Australian Experience*, Melbourne: Oxford University Press.

Faist, T. (2000) *The Volume and Dynamics of International Migration and Transnational Social Spaces*, Oxford: Clarendon.

Flood, J. (1999) *Archaeology of the Dreamtime: The Story of Prehistoric Australia and its People*, revised edn., Pymble, New South Wales: HarperCollins.

Fredrickson, G.M. (1988), "Colonialism and Racism," in *The Arrogance of Race: Historical Perspectives on Slavery, Racism, and Social Inequality*, Hanover: Wesleyan University Press, pp. 216–235.

Galligan, B., Roberts, W. and Trifiletti, G. (2001) *Australians and Globalisation: The Experience of Two Centuries*, Cambridge: Cambridge University Press.

Garnaut, R. (1989) *Australia and the Northeast Asian Ascendency*, Canberra: Australian Government Publishing Service.

Gelder, K. and Jacobs, J.M. (1998) *Uncanny Australia*, Melbourne: Melbourne University Press.

Gellner, E. (1983), *Nations and Nationalism*, Ithaca, New York: Cornell University Press.

—— (1987) *Culture, Identity, and Politics*, Cambridge & London: Cambridge University Press.

Giddens, A. (1990) *The Consequences of Modernity*, Cambridge: Polity Press.

—— (1991) *Modernity and Self-Identity: Self and Society in the Late Modern Age*, Cambridge: Polity Press.

—— (1994) "Living in a Post-Traditional Society," in U. Beck, A. Giddens and S. Lash (eds.), *Reflexive Modernization: Politics, Tradition and Aesthetics in the Modern Social Order*, Cambridge: Polity Press, pp. 56–109.

—— (1999) *Runaway World: BBC Reith Lectures 1999*. Online. http: <http://news.bbc.co.uk/hi/english/static/events/reith_99/default.ht m> (accessed July 31, 2003).

Glazer, N. (1997) *We Are All Multiculturalists Now*, Cambridge, Massachusetts: Harvard University Press.

Goot, M. (1988) "Immigrants and Immigration: Evidence and Arguments from the Polls, 1943–1987," in The Committee to Advice on Australia's Immigration Policies, *Immigration, A Commitment to Australia: Consultants' Reports*, Canberra: Australian Government Publishing Service, Section 1.1.

————— (2001) "Public Opinion on Immigration," in J. Jupp (ed.), *The Australian People: An Encyclopedia of the Nation, its People and Their Origins*, Cambridge: Cambridge University Press, pp. 824–826.

Goot, M. and Rowse, T. (1994) (eds.), *Make A Better Offer: The Politics of Mabo*, Leichhardt: Pluto Press.

Graham, D. (1994) (ed.) *Being Whitefella*, South Fremantle: Fremantle Arts Centre Press.

Gray, I. and Lawrence, G. (2001) *A Future for Regional Australia: Escaping Global Misfortune*, Cambridge: Cambridge University Press.

Guardian Unlimited (2001) "Navy to take Refugees Off Tampa — Court Hearing Delays Move to New Zealand and Nauru," *The Guardian*, Monday, September 3, 2001. Online. http: <http:www.guardian.co.uk/ international/story/0,3604,545799,00.html> (accessed July 11, 2002).

Habermas, J. (1994) "Struggles for Recognition in the Democratic Constitutional State," in A. Gutmann (ed.), *Multiculturalism: Examining the Politics of Recognition*, Princeton, New Jersey: Princeton University Press, pp. 107–148.

————— (2001) *The Postnational Constellation: Political Essays*, Cambridge: Polity Press, pp. 58–112.

Haebich, A. (1992) *For Their Own Good: Aborigines and Government in the South West of Western Australia, 1900–1940*, 2nd edn., Nedlands, Western Australia: University of Western Australia Press.

————— (2000) *Broken Circles: Fragmenting Indigenous Families 1800–2000*, North Fremantle: Fremantle Arts Centre Press.

Hage, G. (1998) *White Nation: Fantasies of White Supremacy in a Multicultural Society*, Sydney: Pluto Press.

Hancock, W.K. (1930) *Australia*, London: Ernest Benn Limited.

Hannerz, U. (1992) *Cultural Complexity: Studies in the Social Organization of Meaning*, New York: Columbia University Press.

————— (1996) *Transnational Connections: Culture, People, Places*, London and New York: Routledge.

Hardy, F. (1978) *The Unlucky Australians*, 2nd edn., London: Pan.

Harris, J. (1990) *One Blood: Two Hundred Years of Aboriginal Encounter with Christianity*, Sutherland, New South Wales: Albatross Books.

Harvey, D. (1989) *The Condition of Postmodernity: An Enquiry into the Origins of Cultural Change*, London: Basil Blackwell.

Havemann, P. (2000) "Enmeshed in the Web? Indigenous Peoples' Rights in the Network Society," in R. Cohen and S.M. Rai (eds.), *Global Social Movements*, London and New Brunswick, New Jersey: The Athlone Press, pp. 18–32.

Hawke, R.J.L. (1994) *The Hawke Memoirs*, Port Melbourne, Victoria: William Heinemann.

Hayward, D. (2002) "The Public Good and the Public Services: What Role for the Private Sector?," *Dissent*, Autumn/Winter: 8–12.

Heelas, P. (1996) "Introduction," in P. Heelas, S. Lash and P. Morris (eds.), *Detraditionalization: Critical Reflections on Authority and Identity*, London: Blackwell.

Heelas, P., Lash, S. and Morris, P. (eds.) (1996) *Detraditionalization: Critical Reflections on Authority and Identity*, London: Blackwell.

Held, D. (1995) *Democracy and the Global Order: From the Modern State to Cosmopolitan Governance*, Cambridge: Polity Press.

Held, D. and McGrew, A. (2000) (eds.) *The Global Transformations Reader*, Cambridge: Polity Press.

Held, D. and McGrew, A. (2002) *Globalization/Anti-Globalization*, Cambridge: Polity Press.

Held, D., McGrew, A., Goldblatt, D. and Perraton, J. (1999) *Global Transformations: Politics, Economics and Culture*, Cambridge: Polity Press.

Hilmer, F. (1993) *National Competition Policy: Report by the Independent Committee of Inquiry*, Canberra: Australian Government Publishing Service.

Hirst, J. (1995) "Australia's Absurd History: A Critique of Multiculturalism (1993)," in J. Lack and J. Templeton (eds.), *Bold Experiment: A Documentary History of Australian Immigration Since 1945*, Melbourne: Oxford University Press, pp. 250–257.

———— (2002) *Australia's Democracy: A Short History*, Crows Nest: Allen & Unwin.

Hirst, P. and Thompson, G. (1995) "Globalization and the Future of the Nation State," *Economy and Society* 24(3): 408–422.

———— (1999) *Globalization in Question: The International Economy and the Possibilities of Governance*, 2nd edn., Cambridge: Polity Press.

Hobsbawm, E. (1990) *Nations and Nationalism Since 1780: Programme, Myth, Reality*, Cambridge and New York: Cambridge University Press.

Holton, R. (1991) "Public Disorder in Australia between 1985 and 1989 with Particular Reference to Immigration and Multiculturalism," *Working*

Papers on Multiculturalism No. 17, Wollongong: Published for The Office of Multicultural Affairs, Department of the Prime Minister and Cabinet, by The Centre for Multicultural Studies, University of Wollongong, Australia.

Hoogvelt, A. (2001) *Globalization and the Postcolonial World: The New Political Economy of Development*, 2nd edn., Basingstoke: Palgrave.

Horne, D. (1964) *The Lucky Country: Australia in the 1960s*, Melbourne: Penguin.

Horner, J. (1974) *Vote Ferguson for Aboriginal Freedom: A Biography*, Sydney: Australian and New Zealand Book Company.

Howard, J. (2001) "Transcript of the Prime Minister The Hon John Howard MP Press Conference," Melbourne, September 3, 2001. Online. http: <http://www.pm.gov.au/news/interviews/2001/interview1211.htm> (accessed July 11, 2002).

Hughes, C. (1973) "Political Culture," in H. Mayer and H. Nelson (eds.), *Australian Politics: A Third Reader*, Melbourne: Cheshire, pp. 133–146.

Human Rights and Equal Opportunity Commission (1997) *Bringing Them Home: Report of the National Inquiry into the Separation of Aboriginal and Torres Strait Islander Children from Their Families* (Commissioner: Sir Ronald Wilson), Sydney: Human Rights and Equal Opportunity Commission.

Inkeles, A. and Levinson, D.J. (1969) "National Character: The Study of Modal Personality and Sociocultural Systems," in G. Lindzey and E. Aronson (eds.), *The Handbook of Social Psychology, Vol. 4*, 2nd edn., Reading, Massachusetts: Addison-Wesley, pp. 418–506.

Irving Saulwick & Associates (2000) *Research into Issues Related to a Document of Reconciliation: A Report Prepared for the Council for Aboriginal Reconciliation*, Canberra: Commonwealth of Australia.

Jamrozik, A. (1994) "From Harvester to De-Regulation: Wage Earners in the Australian Welfare State," *Australian Journal of Social Issues* 29(2): 162–170.

Janke, T. (1998) *Our Culture: Our Future. Report on Australian Indigenous and Intellectual Property Rights*, Canberra: Australian Institute of Aboriginal and Torres Strait Islander Studies.

Jordens, A.-M. (2001) "Post-war non-British Migration," in J. Jupp (ed.), *The Australian People: An Encyclopedia of the Nation, its People and Their Origins*, Cambridge: Cambridge University Press, pp. 65–70.

Joseph, P. (2000) "Maori and the Market: The Waitangi Tribunal," *Race and Class* 41(4): 59–80.

Jupp, J. (1992) "Immigrant Settlement Policy in Australia," in G.P. Freeman and J. Jupp (eds.), *Nations of Immigrants: Australia, the United States, and International Migration*, Melbourne: Oxford University Press, pp. 130–144.

—— (1998) *Immigration*, 2nd edn., Melbourne: Oxford University Press.

—— (2002) *From White Australia to Woomera: The Story of Australian Immigration*, Cambridge: Cambridge University Press.

—— (2003) "There has to be a Better Way: A Long-Term Refugee Strategy," *Australian Fabian Society Pamphlet Number Fifty-Eight*, in Blue Book Number Five, 2003, supplement in Arena Magazine, June–July.

Jupp, J., McRobbie, A. and York, B. (1990) *Metropolitan Ghettoes and Ethnic Concentrations, Vol. 1*, Wollongong: The Centre for Multicultural Studies, University of Wollongong.

Kahn, J.S. (1995) *Culture, Multiculture, Postculture*, London: SAGE.

Kapferer, J. (1990) "Rural Myths and Urban Ideologies," *Australian and New Zealand Journal of Sociology* 26(1): 87–106.

Karpin, P. (1995) *Enterprising Nation: Renewing Australia's Managers to Meet the Challenges of the Asia Pacific Century. Report of the Industry Task Force on Leadership and Management Skills*, Canberra: Australian Government Publishing Service.

Keating, P. (1994) *Working Nation: Policies and Programs*, Canberra: Australian Government Publishing Service.

Kelley, J., Bean, C., Evans, M.D.R. and Zagorski, K. (1996) *National Social Science Survey 1993: Inequality II [computer file]*. Canberra: Social Science Data Archives, The Australian National University.

Kelly, P. (1992) *The End of Certainty: The Story of the 1980s*, St. Leonards: Allen & Unwin.

—— (2001) "Labor and Globalisation," in R. Manne (ed.), *The Australian Century: Political Struggle in the Building of a Nation*, Melbourne: Text, pp. 224–263.

Lack, J. and Templeton, J. (1995) (eds.) *Bold Experiment: A Documentary History of Australian Immigration Since 1945*, Melbourne: Oxford University Press.

Latham, M. (1998) *Civilising Global Capital: New Thinking for Australian Labor*, St. Leonards, New South Wales: Allen & Unwin.

Little, G. (1999) *The Public Emotions: From Mourning to Hope*, Sydney: ABC Books.

Lopez, M. (2000) *The Origins of Multiculturalism in Australian Politics 1945–1975*, Carlton: Melbourne University Press.

Lourandos, H. (1997) *Continent of Hunter-Gatherers: New Perspectives in Australian Prehistory*, New York: Cambridge University Press.

MacCallum, M. (2002) *Girt By Sea: Australia, the Refugees and the Politics of Fear*, *Quarterly Essay*, Issue 5, Melbourne: Black Inc.

Macintyre, S. and Clark, A. (2003) *The History Wars*, Carlton, Victoria: Melbourne University Press.

Mackay, H. (1993) *Reinventing Australia: The Mind and Mood of Australia in the 90s*, Sydney: Angus & Robertson.

―――― (1997) *Generations: Baby Boomers, Their Parents and Their Children*, Sydney: Macmillan.

―――― (2001) *Mind & Mood*, Report No. 100, New South Wales: Mackay Research Limited.

Maddox, G. (1998) "The Australian Settlement and Australian Political Thought," in P. Smyth and B. Cass (eds.), *Contesting the Australian Way*, Cambridge: Cambridge University Press, pp. 57–68.

Manne, R. (2001) "A Little Boy Lost in the Lucky Country," *Sydney Morning Herald*, Monday, August 27, 2001.

―――― (2003) (ed.) *Whitewash: On Keith Windschuttle's Fabrication of Aboriginal History*, Melbourne: Black Inc.

Mares, P. (2002) *Borderline: Australia's Response to Refugees and Asylum Seekers in the Wake of the Tampa*, revised edn., Sydney: UNSW Press.

Markus, A. (1988) "How Australians See Each Other," in The Committee to Advise on Australia's Immigration Policies, *Immigration, A Commitment to Australia: Consultants' Reports*, Canberra: Australian Government Publishing Service, Section 1.3.

Marr, D. and Wilkinson, M. (2003) *Dark Victory*, Crows Nest, New South Wales: Allen & Unwin.

Martin, J. (1978) *The Migrant Presence: Australian Responses 1947–1977. Research Report for the National Population Inquiry*, Sydney: George Allen & Unwin.

Maybury-Lewis, D. (1997) *Indigenous Peoples, Ethnic Groups, and the State*, Boston: Allyn and Bacon.

McCalman, J. (1993) *Journeyings: The Biography of a Middle-Class Generation 1920–1990*, Melbourne: Melbourne University Press.

McGregor, R. (1997) *Imagined Destinies: Aboriginal Australians and the Doomed Race Theory, 1880–1939*, Carlton: Melbourne University Press.

McMaster, D. (2001) *Asylum Seekers: Australia's Response to Refugees*, Melbourne: Melbourne University Press.

Meredith, D. and Dyster, B. (1999) *Australia in the Global Economy: Continuity and Change*, Cambridge/Melbourne: Cambridge University Press.

Miller, D. (1993) "In Defence of Nationality," *Journal of Applied Philosophy* 10(1): 3–16.

——— (1995) *On Nationality*, Oxford: Clarendon Press.

Ministerial Statements (2001) "Illegal Immigration: MV Tampa, Mr Howard (Bennelong – Prime Minister) 2 pm, 29 August 2001," Australian Department of Foreign Affairs and Trade. Online. http: <http://www.dfat.gov.au/media/tampa_ms290801.html> (accessed July 11, 2002).

Mitchell, A. and Bassanese, D. (2003) "Economic Reform: A Barrel of Thrills and Spills," in S. Ryan and Troy Bramston (eds.), *The Hawke Government: A Critical Perspective*, North Melbourne, Victoria: Pluto Press, pp. 131–139.

Moody, R. (1988a) (ed.) *The Indigenous Voice: Visions and Realities, Vol.* 1, London: Zed Books.

——— (1988b) (ed.) *The Indigenous Voice: Visions and Realities, Vol.* 2, London: Zed Books.

Moran, A. (1998) "Aboriginal Reconciliation: Transformations in Settler Nationalism," *Melbourne Journal of Politics* 25: 101–131.

Mulvaney, D.J. (1957) "The Australian Aborigines 1606–1929: Opinion and Fieldwork, Part 1," *Historical Studies Australia and New Zealand* 8(29): 131–151.

Nagel, J. (1997) *American Indian Ethnic Revival: Red Power and the Resurgence of Identity and Culture*, New York and London: Oxford University Press.

National Multicultural Advisory Council (1999) *Australian Multiculturalism for a New Century: Towards Inclusiveness*, Canberra: Department of Immigration and Multicultural Affairs. Available Online. http: <http://www.immi.gov.au> (accessed October 10, 2003).

Newspoll Market Research (2000) *Quantitative Research into Issues Relating to a Document of Reconciliation: Summary of Findings. Prepared for the Council for Aboriginal Reconciliation*, Canberra: Commonwealth of Australia.

Niezen, R. (2000) "Recognizing Indigenism: Canadian Unity and the International Movement of Indigenous Peoples," *Comparative Studies in Society and History* 42(1): 119–148.

O'Connor, K., Stimson, R. and Daly, M. (2001) *Australia's Changing Economic Geography: A Society Dividing*, South Melbourne: Oxford University Press.

Osborne, D. and Gaebler, T. (1992) *Reinventing Government*, New York: Addison-Wesley.

Paolini, A.J. (1999) *Navigating Modernity: Postcolonialism, Identity and International Relations*, Boulder, Colorado: Lynne Rienner Publishers.

Parkin, A. and Hardcastle, L. (1997) "Immigration and Ethnic Affairs Policy," in D. Woodward, A. Parkin and J. Summers (eds.), *Government, Politics, Power and Policy in Australia*, 6th edn., South Melbourne: Longman, pp. 486–509.

Peel, M. (2003) *The Lowest Rung: Voices of Australian Poverty*, Cambridge: Cambridge University Press.

Perry, R.J. (1996) *From Time Immemorial: Indigenous Peoples and State Systems*, Austin: University of Texas Press.

Phillips, T. (1998) "Popular Views About Australian Identity: Research and Analysis," *Journal of Sociology* 34(3): 281–302.

Phillips, T. and Smith, P. (2000) "What is 'Australian?' Knowledge and Attitudes Among a Gallery of Contemporary Australians," *Australian Journal of Political Science* 35(2): 203–224.

Pusey, M. (1991) *Economic Rationalism in Canberra: A Nation Building State Changes its Mind*, Cambridge: Cambridge University Press.

—— (2003) *The Experience of Middle Australia: The Dark Side of Economic Reform*, Melbourne: Cambridge University Press.

Pye, L. (1968) "Political Culture," *International Encyclopaedia of the Social Sciences*, Vol. 12, New York: Macmillan, pp. 218–225.

Read, P. (1990) "Cheeky, Insolent and Anti-White: The Split in the Federal Council for Advancement of Aborigines and Torres Strait Islanders — Easter 1970," *The Australian Journal of Politics and History* 36(1): 73–83.

—— (2000) *Belonging: Australians, Place and Aboriginal Ownership*, Oakleigh, Victoria: Cambridge University Press.

Reconciliation and Social Justice Library (2003) Online. http: <http://www.austlii.edu.au/au/special/rsjproject/rsjlibrary/car>

Reich, R.B. (1991) *The Work of Nations*, New York: Knopf.

Reynolds, H. (1987) *Frontier: Aborigines, Settlers and Land*, Sydney: Allen & Unwin.

—— (1989) (Compiler) *Dispossession: Black Australians and White Invaders*, Sydney: Allen & Unwin.

—— (1990) *The Other Side of the Frontier: Aboriginal Resistance to the European Invasion of Australia*, revised edn., Ringwood: Penguin.

——— (1998) *This Whispering in Our Hearts*, St. Leonards, New South Wales: Allen & Unwin.

——— (2003) *North of Capricorn: The Untold Story of Australia's North*, Crows Nest, New South Wales: Allen & Unwin.

Rivett, K. (2001) "Refugees," in J. Jupp (ed.), *The Australian People: An Encyclopedia of the Nation, its People and Their Origins*, Cambridge: Cambridge University Press, pp. 829–834.

Robertson, R. (1995) "Glocalization: Time-Space and Homogeneity-Heterogeneity," in M. Featherstone, S. Lash and R. Robertson (eds.), *Global Modernities*, London: Sage, chap. 2.

Rosenberg, J. (2000) *The Follies of Globalisation Theory: Polemical Essays*, London: Verso.

Rowley, C. (1972) *The Destruction of Aboriginal Society*, Melbourne: Penguin Books.

Roy Morgan Research (2001) "'Refugees Not Welcome' Australians Say," Roy Morgan International Poll, Finding No. 3446, published in *The Bulletin*, September 25, 2001. Online. http: <http:www.roymorgan.com/news/ polls/2001/ 3446/index.cfm> (accessed September 3, 2003).

Ruddock, P. (2002) *Background Paper on Unauthorised Arrivals Strategy*. Media release from Phillip Ruddock MP, Minister for Immigration, Multicultural and Indigenous Affairs. Online. http: <http://www.minister.immi.gov.au/media_releases/ med.../r01131-bgpaper.ht> (accessed July 11, 2002).

Sanders, D. (1980) "The Formation of the World Council of Indigenous Peoples," Center for World Indigenous Studies. Online. http: <http://www. cwis.org/fwdp/International/wcipinfo.txt> (accessed October 17, 2002).

Sassen, S. (1998) *Globalization and its Discontents: Essays on the New Mobility of People and Money*, New York: The New Press.

Schedvin, C.B. (1987) "The Australian Economy on the Hinge of History," *The Australian Economic Review* 1(77): 20–30.

Schlesinger Jr., A.M. (1992) *The Disuniting of America*, New York: Norton.

Senate Select Committee on a Certain Maritime Incident (2002) *Report of the Senate Select Committee on a Certain Maritime Incident*, Canberra: Commonwealth of Australia.

Sennett, R. (1998) *The Corrosion of Character: The Personal Consequences of Work in the New Capitalism*, London/New York: Norton.

Sharp, N. (1996) *No Ordinary Judgment: Mabo, the Murray Islanders' Land Case*, Canberra: Aboriginal Studies Press.

Simons, M. (2003) *The Meeting of the Waters: The Hindmarsh Island Affair*, Sydney: Hodder.

Sklair, L. (2001) *The Transnational Capitalist Class*, London: Blackwell.

Smith, A.D. (1987) *The Ethnic Origins of Nations*, Oxford UK/New York, NY: Basil Blackwell.

Smith, A.D. (1993) "The Nation: Invented, Imagined, Reconstructed," in M. Ringrose and A.J. Lerner (eds.), *Reimagining the Nation*, Buckingham: Open University Press, chap. 1.

——— (1995) *Nations and Nationalism in the Global Era*, Cambridge: Polity Press.

Smith, B. (1969) *European Vision and the South Pacific, 1768–1850*, London: Oxford University Press.

Smith, C. and Ward, G.K. (2000) (eds.) *Indigenous Cultures in an Interconnected World*, St. Leonards, New South Wales: Allen & Unwin.

Smith, R. (2001) *Australian Political Culture*, Frenchs Forest, New South Wales: Pearson Education, Longman.

Stanner, W.E.H. (1979) "Continuity and Change Among the Aborigines (1958)," in *White Man Got No Dreaming: Essays 1938–1973*, Canberra: Australian National University Press, pp. 41–66.

Tacey, D.J. (1995) *Edge of the Sacred: Transformation in Australia*, Blackburn North, Victoria: HarperCollins.

The Independent Commission on International Humanitarian Issues (1987) *Indigenous Peoples: A Global Quest for Justice. A Report for the Independent Commission on International Humanitarian Issues*, London and New Jersey: Zed Books.

Thompson, E. (1994) *Fair Enough: Egalitarianism in Australia*, Sydney: UNSW Press.

Tully, J. (1995) *Strange Multiplicity: Constitutionalism in an Age of Diversity*, Cambridge: Cambridge University Press.

Tyler, H. (2003) *Asylum: Voices Behind the Razor Wire*, South Melbourne: Lothian Books.

United Nations High Commissioner for Refugees (2000), *The State of the World's Refugees: Fifty Years of Humanitarian Action*, Oxford: Oxford University Press.

United Nations Office of the High Commissioner for Human Rights (1999) *Decision 2 (54) on Australia, Committee on the Elimination of Racial*

Discrimination, Fifty-Fourth session. Online. http: <http://www.unhchr.ch/tbs> (accessed September 26, 2003).

U.S. Committee for Refugees (2002), *Sea Change: Australia's New Approach to Asylum Seekers*, Washington: USCR.

Walsh, M. (1979) *Poor Little Rich Country: The Path to the Eighties*, Ringwood, Victoria: Penguin Books.

Ward, R. (1966) *The Australian Legend*, 2nd edn., Oxford: Oxford University Press.

Watson, D. (2002) *Recollections of a Bleeding Heart: A Portrait of Paul Keating PM*, Milsons Point: Knopf.

Watts, R. (1980) "The Origins of the Australian Welfare State," *Historical Studies* 19(75): 175–198.

Webber, J. (1994) *Reimagining Canada: Language, Culture, Community, and the Canadian Constitution*, Kingston and Montreal: McGill-Queen's University Press.

Weiss, L. (1998) *The Myth of the Powerless State: Governing the Economy in the Global Era*, Cambridge: Polity Press.

White, C. (1992) "Mastering Risk: The Story of Australian Economic Success," in J. Carroll and R. Manne (eds.), *Shutdown: The Failure of Economic Rationalism and How to Rescue Australia*, Melbourne: Text, pp. 27–37.

Wilmer, F. (1993) *The Indigenous Voice in World Politics: Since Time Immemorial*, Newbury Park, California: Sage.

Windschuttle, K. (2002) *The Fabrication of Aboriginal History*, Vol. 1, Paddington, New South Wales: Macleay Press.

Yunupingu, G. (1998) "We Know These Things to Be True," The 3rd Vincent Lingiari Memorial Lecture Delivered by Galarrwuy Yunupingu, AM, Chairman of the Northern Land Council, August 20, 1998, Northern Territory University, Reconciliation and Justice Library. Online. http: http://www.austlii.edu.au/au/special/rsjproject/rsjlibrary/car/lingiari/3yunupingu.htm (accessed November 6, 2003).

Index

debates about, 19–23
definition of, 7
history of, in Australia, 2
as ideology, 29, 33–34
intensified processes of, 34
and large scale movements of
    people, 9–10, 18–19
and nation-state, national
    identity, 21
and regions, 20
special meaning of, for
    Australians, 5–6
and the state, 21–23
and stretching of political
    community, 174–175
theories of, 19–20
as a threat for Australians, 31–32
western-centric globalization, 143
Governance
Australian form of, 1
Australian government and
    globalization, 16, 105
global, 21, 34, 175, 179–180,
    185, 211
and global market assessment, 29
intergovernmental agreements, 22
Guantanamo Bay, 7

H

Habermas, Jürgen, 118
Hancock, W. K., 23–26, 44, 46
Hannerz, Ulf, 5, 21, 54–55
Hanson, Pauline
    and Aborigines, 129
    and "Asianization" of Australia,
        116

and One Nation Party, 116
and threat to Australia's cultural,
    trade and security links with
    Asia, 208–209
Harris, John, 161
Harvester Judgement, 24
Havemann, Paul, 159
Hawke, Bob (former Australian
    Prime Minister)
    and Aboriginal rights, 167
Hawke government,
    and Council for Aboriginal
        Reconciliation, 168
    and creation of APEC, 32
    disparaging remarks about
        asylum seekers, 187
    and engagement with Asia,
        115–116
    multicultural policy of, 110–112
    and multicultural, cosmopolitan
        Australian identity, 33, 115
    and restructuring of Australia, 3
Heelas, Paul, 35
Held, David, 1, 7, 19, 32
Henry (interviewee), 97–99
Hirst, John, 42, 120–121
Hirst, Paul, 19
Hobsbawm, Eric, 81
Horne, Donald, 51
Howard, John, (Australian Prime
    Minister), 181
    and border protection, 8
    comments on Asian immigration
        when opposition leader 99, 115
    criticism of asylum seekers, 188,
        199